D1458194

MANTLES AND MATCHES

MANTLES AND MATCHES

A Hertfordshire Childhood

by
Molly Eldrett, née Kitchener

ARTHUR H. STOCKWELL LTD
Torrs Park   Ilfracombe   Devon
Established 1898
www.ahstockwell.co.uk

British Library Cataloguing-in-Publication Data.
A catalogue record for this book is available
from the British Library.

ISBN 978-0-7223-4020-2
Printed in Great Britain by
Arthur H. Stockwell Ltd
Torrs Park   Ilfracombe
Devon

Dedicated to my grandchildren,
who encouraged me to remember.

Acknowledgements

The author and publishers are grateful to the following for permission to reproduce photographs:
Hitchin Museum;
The Comet newspaper, Hitchin.

Every effort has been made to acknowledge the correct copyright holders and the publishers will, if notified, correct any errors or omissions in future editions.

CONTENTS

Introduction	9
In the Beginning	11
My Family	18
Hitchin, My Hometown	26
Making Ends Meet	37
The Cold Place	43
The First Siren	49
Educating Molly	55
An Unforgettable Character	65
When Father Papered the Parlour	71
Happiness Is Sunday Tea	77
An Afternoon Out	83
Going to Camp	89
Praise the Lord!	94
A Really Lovely Holiday	101
Time to Grow Up	108

Introduction

I first got the idea to write about my childhood after talking to two of my grandchildren, then aged seven and three, as they recovered from chickenpox. It was good to have a captive audience. They seemed really interested in quite ordinary things that had happened during my childhood, like when I climbed the old apple tree in the garden, picked an apple and settled down to spend an hour curled up in the branches with my cat, Chummy, reading a book. It made me stop and ask myself, 'How has life changed for today's children, and is it for the better?' How many children spend time outside as we did, climbing trees, exploring, or paddling in local streams?

Today we take for granted things like television, washing machines, videos, vacuum cleaners, dishwashers, computers and mobile phones, but in the 1940s these things were not part of an ordinary household. Housework was hard, manual labour and it occupied most of the day.

Life for everyone has changed out of all recognition during the past sixty years – not only in the home, but at work and play. Equality of opportunity for women means that more mothers are able to go out to work, and pressure from advertising means that it is now very important to earn enough money to buy luxuries. Peer pressure from both adults and children is overwhelming.

I have started to think about ordinary things that happened in my childhood, and I feel that they are important enough to write down for my grandchildren to read.

This is not a story about a rich family, but about ordinary people in Hertfordshire in the 1930s and 1940s, living on the edge of a war which was to change the world.

It is easy to say, "Those were the days!" Looking back, we often remember happy times and nostalgia takes over. We forget that a lot of the time was spent working hard in difficult conditions, but for me it really was a very happy childhood.

In the Beginning

Twenty-nine Ickleford Road, Hitchin, Hertfordshire was my home for the first twenty-one years of my life. A Victorian terraced house in the centre of a small market town, it was the place that sheltered me during my childhood.

The back door was reached from the street through a narrow passageway between our house and next door. Our bedrooms were built over this passage, making them larger than our neighbours', giving us a feeling of superiority. The passageway offered a sheltered place for that goodnight peck from our shy

boyfriends, interrupted after five minutes by Dad putting out the milk bottles.

"Time you were indoors!" he would say. "It's ten o'clock."

Just inside the back door was the scullery – a small, rather dark room with its red quarry-tiled floor, softened only by a multicoloured rag rug made out of the family's old coats. Walls were distempered in green, and the white of the ceiling was stained by fumes from the gaslight and coal smoke from the copper.

There was no electricity in the house and very few modern conveniences.

In one corner of the scullery was a brownstone sink with a brass tap above. No hot water came out of this polished protrusion. Next to the sink a copper set in brickwork with a wooden lid heated the water for Monday washdays. Mum used to get up at six o'clock to light the coal fire under the copper. Water would be fetched in from the water butt in the garden in an old pail, and as soon as it reached boiling point all the whites were put in – sheets, pillowcases, handkerchiefs, school blouses and Dad's shirts. These were left to boil in the copper, aided by a few prods from the wooden tongs. Coloureds were washed by hand in the sink using soda crystals to soften the water and flakes of soap to rub them clean.

After this the washing was rinsed, the whites dipped in water with a blue bag added, and then everything was put through a wooden mangle. Then, and only then, could it be hung out in the garden to dry. Wet Mondays were very bad news for everyone, as all the washing would have to be dried indoors, making every room feel cold and damp. Monday dinner time my sister, Jean, and I came home from school to help Mum fold the sheets. Mum took in washing to bring a few coppers into our home – towels from the local council offices, shirts and sheets from a better-off family who lived in one of the posh roads nearby.

It was Jean's and my job to collect and deliver the washing, and this provided us with the only pocket money we had.

Once a week – Fridays – the copper was lit once more for bath night. Again the water was collected from the water butt and carried into the scullery. The tin bath was brought in from the barn, and the water was transferred, again by bucket, into the copper. Jean and I bathed first, then Mum, then my Dad if he was home from work. Needless to say, the four inches of water allowed during the war was not too clean when it came to Dad's turn. After we had bathed, the water was scooped out into a bowl and thrown away, down the sink. The bath was scoured clean and taken back to the barn, and my sister and I were given our weekly dose of syrup of figs. Ugh!

The whole operation was really hard work for us all, and I wonder if we were any cleaner after the bath was emptied and returned to the barn and the fire under the copper cleaned out.

Along the back wall of the scullery were shelves, housing basins, saucepans and plates. Under the shelves stood a wooden table scrubbed clean daily until it was almost white. This table was the centre of all the cooking preparations. A meat safe was nailed to the wall, housing meat, milk, butter, bacon and anything fresh which needed to be kept cool. In the hot weather, milk was stood in a bowl of cold water. The iron mangle stood next to the back door. The scullery was not light and airy, like modern kitchens, but dark, damp and usually cold. On washdays it smelled of soapsuds and disinfectant.

Although the room was not inviting, it was the centre of much activity – usually centred on my mother. It alternated between smells of cooking, washing, coal and wood smoke, and when my father was mending our shoes it smelt of leather and leather dye. I have happy memories of my father teaching me to skin and clean rabbits for the pot and to pluck chickens in the scullery. What a mess that made!

The living room was the main room of the house, and it was dominated by a large black iron range – nice and warm in winter; overpowering in summer. The range was blackleaded by Mum every morning. As this was the only means of cooking, it was lit every day. A large black kettle always sat boiling on top, joined by saucepans prior to mealtimes and black flat irons following washday. Eventually the range was replaced by an open fire, and a gas stove was installed in the scullery for cooking.

A large deal table took up most of the room with four wooden chairs tucked underneath. Only my father had an armchair. The arms were wooden, it was not very comfortable, and we weren't allowed to sit in it. A wireless took pride of place by the window and an ottoman was our sickbed in times of illness. The floor was covered with linoleum and the room was lit by gaslight. A cupboard under the stairs served as our pantry and doubled up as a bedroom for my sister and me during air raids. A small cupboard next to the range held linen and china.

The front room was our holy of holies – only used on high days and holidays. It was dominated by two large black leather chairs with a matching sofa. These were very cold to sit on, very uncomfortable and smelled of leather polish. The front door opened on to the front garden, so there was always a draught blowing in. This entrance was only used on special occasions, such as weddings and funerals and when the doctor called. An old brown blanket hung across the door. Two large black-framed pictures decorated the walls. I seem to remember that one was a scene of Highland cattle and the other of stags at bay, but my main recollection is of those awful black frames.

Steep stairs rose through the centre of the house; a narrow stair carpet was held in place by brass stair rods, which my sister and I had to clean every Saturday along with all the brass ornaments and silver cutlery.

My parents' bedroom was at the front of the house, with a large iron and brass bedstead in the centre. The mattress was filled with feathers, which had to be shaken and rearranged every day. There was no wardrobe or cupboard; just a huge chest of drawers, smelling of lavender, and a washstand with a marble top and cupboards underneath. A blue and white jug and basin was provided for washing purposes.

I shared not only a bedroom but a bed with my sister – again an iron bedstead with brass bedknobs which unscrewed and made a great hiding place for sweets and chewing gum. Our only furniture was a washbasin with the obligatory jug. There was no heating at all, and the gaslights were only used on special occasions. Candles were our only form of lighting. Linoleum on the floor made for very cold feet.

When my sister or I were unwell and the doctor was called we were moved swiftly into the front bedroom. The doctor was never allowed to visit us in the back room. Chamber pots sat under both beds, and they had to be emptied each morning. My sister and I invented a game of boxing on our bed. Sheets were tied to the bedknobs – these were the ropes. We each had our own corner and an imaginary whistle would start each bout. "Come out fighting," we would call out, and the boxing match would commence. It was all good fun, but we both knew that sooner or later Dad would come roaring up the stairs, puffing and blowing, and we would both get a good hiding. Looking back, it was a no-win situation.

"What did you do if you needed the toilet in the night?" my granddaughter asked me once.

"Use the pot under the bed," I replied, "and empty it in the morning."

"Ugh – I couldn't do that," she shuddered.

"You would if there was no alternative," I told her.

A very small room at the back of the house was used by my grandmother from Welwyn Garden City when she came to stay – usually when she had fallen out with her son, with whom she lived.

The house boasted no bathroom – the lavatory was housed in an old barn up the garden. It was freezing in the winter and very scary during air raids. There was no privacy in the lavatory, which was just a space partitioned off with no door. Next to the lavatory was the coal pile, and on the other side my father's workbench. Bicycles stood along one wall and the tin bath hung from its nail on another. The lavatory was built of white wood and looked like a box with a hole in the middle. Toilet paper was cut-up pages of a telephone directory hung on a piece of string.

The front garden was about six feet square with a low privet hedge and periwinkle flowers – nothing else. The back garden was much nicer – quite large and bounded on the north side by an eight-foot brick wall. This made the garden sheltered, and my father spent hours outside digging, hoeing, planting and weeding. He was an enthusiastic gardener, but he would only grow vegetables.

"What do you want to grow flowers for?" he would say. "You can't eat flowers."

I can still see him digging the plot, with a Woodbine hanging out of the side of his mouth and braces holding up his tattered trousers. He grew a large variety of vegetables, and as a child I thought that it was magic when the tiny green shoots peeped through the dark earth. Raspberry and loganberry canes produced wonderful fruit, as did the apple and Victoria-plum tree. We were never short of fresh food, and my sister and I were kept busy shelling the peas and chopping up mint for the mint sauce. During the war Dad kept chickens in a run near to the barn, so eggs were usually plentiful.

A very small piece of ground, about eight foot square, was left uncultivated. This we proudly called our grass. This was no velvet lawn, but weeds and grasses cut with a pair of scissors. Next to the grass I had persuaded Dad to give me a small piece of ground of my own.

"I suppose you want to grow flowers," he grumbled. "What's wrong with vegetables?"

"Please, Dad!" I was close to tears. "I really want to grow flowers. They are so much prettier than vegetables."

Dad gave in. I knew how to get round him, and it was here that my love of gardening was born, encouraged by our neighbour, Mr Furr. He taught me how to grow flowers and to put some colour into our garden. Under the apple tree Dad allowed a wonderful bed of lilies of the valley to flourish. In the spring this created a sea of nodding white bells and a perfume which was indescribable. Nothing else would grow in the shade of the tree, so they were allowed to stay undisturbed.

During the war an Anderson shelter was installed close to the house. It was only used a couple of times as a shelter. We preferred to stay indoors during air raids, so we used the shelter as our playroom – but only during the summer. During the winter the shelter usually had a foot of water swilling around the floor, so it was not ideal as a safe place to shelter in.

One of my favourite memories is of summer Sunday afternoons, curled up in the gnarled branches of our ancient apple tree with Chummy, my cat, next to me, a book in one hand and an apple plucked from the tree in the other. What could be more peaceful? I dreaded the moment when Mum would call out from the scullery:

"Have you finished your homework? It's almost time for tea."

Although our home was not grand, and was often cold and dark, it holds warm memories for me. I spent wonderful evenings playing bagatelle with Mum and Dad and my sister, and at Christmas with our aunts and grandmother, around the fire in the front room. There would be paper chains hanging from the ceiling and a rather battered Christmas tree, which was dug up every year. The blackouts would be in place. I look back with fond memories, but we were all pleased when electricity came to 29 Ickleford Road. What a difference that made!

My Family

"What were your mum and dad like?" my granddaughter frequently asked. "Were they strict? Where did you live and where did your dad work? Did you see your grandparents often?"

Such questions started me thinking, and as I recalled my childhood I began to realise just how different my parents and grandparents lives were compared with those of today's families.

My mother was born in 1902 in Rotherhythe in the East End of London. Her father, a dock labourer, died when he was in his thirties and before his youngest child was born. He was a local Methodist preacher and, according to my mother, a very hard man. He was tough on discipline, and Mum had a very hard time as a child, especially as she was the eldest daughter in a family of four boys and two girls and had to help Granny Foster with the housework and take care of the younger children.

After my grandfather's death, the family moved to Hitchin, where my parents met. In 1924 they were married in St Mary's Church. After Mum's marriage, her family moved to Welwyn Garden City – a beautiful town where every house had a garden surrounded by hedges. It really was a green place. Granny Foster was the most loving and cuddly person in the world. Her round face was always smiling. She was amply built, her lap always available for us to snuggle on to. As a mother of six children, she must have had a hard life bringing them up alone after Granddad died, but I never heard her grumble.

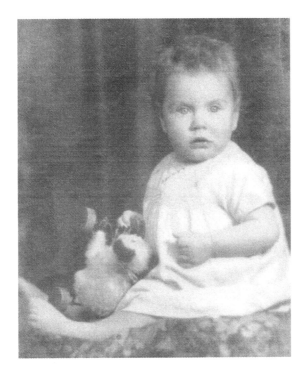

Me, aged nine months.

Dad with Jean and me.

Mum, Auntie May and me.

Mum, Jean and me.

Jean and me.

Mum, Jean and me.

St Mary's Church, Hitchin, where my parents were married.

Four of Gran's children lived close by in Welwyn Garden City. Only Mum and Uncle Fred had remained in Hitchin. We visited Gran about twice a year, and these visits were real treats. We would walk to Hitchin Station and board the steam train, excited at the prospect of the day ahead. We would count the stations where the train would stop – Stevenage, Knebworth, Welwyn North and finally Welwyn Garden City. Excitedly we would jump down on to the station platform, and the huge Shredded Wheat factory would loom up over all the other buildings. We walked the mile or so to Gran's and then the day would stretch out in front of us.

Next door to Gran lived her son Jack, his wife, Auntie Sylv, and daughters, Joan and Ivy. Jean and I were a bit frightened of Auntie Sylv, but Uncle Jack, a night-time GPO telephonist, was like Gran – loving and friendly.

I always remember visiting their home when we were at Gran's. There was a sideboard in the living room – something that Mum and Dad couldn't afford – and the house, which was owned by the council, also boasted electric light, a bathroom and hot water. The sideboard was the real attraction as it held a large bowl of fruit for all to see. There were apples, bananas, grapes, pears and oranges, all in pristine condition, ripe and mouth-watering. Jean and I always dreamed of being offered something from this bowl, but we never tasted the delights.

"Isn't Auntie Sylv mean!" we would whisper to each other. "She might offer us an apple or a pear."

It wasn't until we were adults that the truth emerged – they were all artificial. I wish we had known that as children – we would have thought more kindly of Auntie Sylv.

"What about your dad's family?" The questions kept coming. "Where did they live? Are any of them still alive?" I thought back to my father's family. How different they were to my mother's! They all lived in Hitchin, and, with the exception of one aunt, they remained in the town until they died. Granny Kitchener was a rather austere lady – not soft and cuddly. I always remember her as head of the household, and our aunts, uncles and cousins obeyed her without question. Of her daughters, Glad and Queenie remained unmarried, but Gwen married Uncle Bob, a handsome Royal Marine. Auntie May, a close friend of Auntie Glad, was brought up as a daughter. George (my father) and Horace, known as Odge, were the sons.

Granddad Kitchener, a painter and decorator, seemed to me to be an outsider. He was never included in family gatherings, but was always in the company of his beloved dog, Cody. I remember that after he died, Gran and my aunts would visit the cemetery every Saturday with large bunches of flowers which they placed on his grave. I always thought that they could have been more loving to him when he was alive. The worst memory I have of my grandfather was being taken to see him lying in his coffin in the front room of his house and having to kiss him goodbye. I can still recall the clammy feel of his skin – I could only have been about five years old.

My father was a mixture of good and not so good. He had a quick temper; and if Jean and I were arguing over a toy, he would snatch it from us and throw it into the fire. There would be no discussion, just quick action, and the problem would be solved. On the other hand he would give us little treats – sweets, apples, the odd penny . . . But best of all were the cycling trips. We would explore the Hertfordshire countryside and pick bluebells in Preston Woods by the armful. They would be almost dead when we finally reached home. Pegston Hills were another favourite destination, and we would climb the chalky hills. The views at the top were wonderful. We would look out over miles of beautiful Hertfordshire countryside; the village houses clustered around the tiny churches looked like dolls' houses. Sometimes we would walk alongside the river at Oughtonhead; and if we were really lucky and it was Sunday, we might call in at the George Inn at Ickleford for a glass of lemonade.

Mum was a quiet lady – a wonderful cook, needlewoman and homemaker. Her sole aim in life was to care for us all.

Sadly Dad died aged sixty-five from lung cancer, aggravated by being gassed in France in the First World War. Mum lived to the ripe old age of eighty-seven – the last three years spent in a residential home in a village near Hitchin. Although we remembered her as a quiet lady, at the rest home she was lively and challenging to say the least. Once when the local vicar called he asked the residents if they would like to join in his service.

After Mum had told him in no uncertain terms what she thought of his invitation, he patted her on the head saying, "Bless you, my child," and moved quickly on.

Jean was ten and a half months older than me. She was born in January 1933, and I followed in December of the same year. This caused confusion and embarrassment when Mum had to renew our ration books at the local food office.

"You've put the wrong year down, love!" the clerk would exclaim in a loud voice. "They can't have both been born in the same year."

Mum would then have to explain the facts quietly and the ration books would be issued. Then, red-faced, she would have to pass by a queue of housewives muttering and tittering amongst themselves.

Jean and I were very different in appearance. Jean was small with dark-brown hair and brown eyes, like Dad; and I was tall with fair curly hair and blue eyes, like Mum. We could never have been mistaken for twins. Our characters were very different, as I will record in later chapters.

Looking back, I realise how lucky we were to have such a loving family surrounding us. When I visit Hitchin I usually try to visit St Mary's Church, where it all began. It sits there as a lasting monument to a very happy childhood.

Hitchin, My Hometown

I was born in the market town of Hitchin, and the places where we played and went to school we took for granted. It is only now, whilst writing an account of my childhood, that I realise just what an interesting town Hitchin was – and still is.

Road names, familiar to us as children, were just that – road names. Now I find interesting stories about many of them and would like to find out more. Tilehouse Street, where my great-grandmother ran the Old Bull's Head pub, takes its name from the tile kilns that once existed there. Duke's Lane, which we walked daily on our way to Wilshere-Dacre School was at one time known as Dyke's Lane. Perhaps years earlier it was connected to the River Hiz, which runs through the town.

Hitchin in the 1930s was a very different place from what it is now.

Jean and I were born in the front bedroom of 29 Ickleford Road. This road consisted mainly of rented terraced houses, the first of which was built during the 1860s. Later a few semis were added, and gradually the number of houses increased to 100. The owners of Moss's, a large grocer's shop in the town, owned some of the houses and let them to their employees. There were also two police houses next to the Picturedrome, later called Blakes, which was built in 1911. I understand it was one of the first purpose-built cinemas in the country. During our childhood it stood empty. I can never remember it being open to the public. Opposite Blakes, on the corner of Bunyan Road, stood The Victoria, an old public house. I recall timidly knocking on the door of the back room, jug in hand.

"Can you fill this jug for my dad?" I would ask, and then I'd carry it carefully home, trying hard not to spill any.

There were three shops in Ickleford Road during our childhood. Studman's, the post office, was at one end and sold sweets, newspapers and stationery. Our friends, Pam and June Studman, lived behind the shop. Tart's was a tiny grocer's shop run by Peg Tart and her mother in the front room of a tiny Victorian terraced house, reached by a flight of steep steps. I remember going there with Jean for a jug of vinegar and drinking some on the way home.

"I'll go indoors and talk to Mum," I'd tell Jean, "and you go into the scullery and fill the jug with water. Mum won't know."

Opposite our house was the dairy. The horse that pulled the milk cart was stabled behind the shop.

Ickleford Road joined Bancroft, one of Hitchin's main streets, and it was here that I saw our own Queen Mother, accompanied by her two young daughters, Princess Elizabeth and Princess Margaret Rose, emerging from an antiques shop. The Queen Mother, then our queen, had a home at St Paul's Walden, a village nearby.

There was much excitement every other year when Mum had saved up enough money and clothing coupons to buy us a new coat or a pair of shoes. Jumpers were always knitted by Mum, and dresses were made out of either her old dresses or one of my aunts'. Nicholl's, Morris's and Spurr's were the main department stores in the town. Spurr's was our favourite as there were two or three floors to explore. Nicholl's was rather old-fashioned and had three or four uninspiring window displays, but we were always fascinated when the sales assistant packed our money into a metal container and pulled the string. The container would sail away over our heads en route to the cashier's office, and it would be returned complete with change and a receipt. As small children, this was as exciting as flying to the moon would be nowadays.

Morris's was the most modern store. It had a very good department selling baby clothes – goods which interested Jean and me when we had young families. Nursery goods, such as prams and high chairs, could be bought in Munt's in the High Street, which also sold toys and bicycles. I still remember the bare wooden floor with its own peculiar smell. Perks & Llewellyn's opposite always smelled of lavender and lavender products, gathered from the lavender fields to the west of the town. Huge jars holding coloured liquids were displayed in the windows.

The High Street also housed Woolworth's – a popular shop selling affordable wares. Dad bought pieces of leather to mend our shoes from the hardware counter, but my favourite was usually a bag of broken biscuits. Sadly none of these shops has survived.

The place where my sister and I spent most of our spare time was Bancroft Recreation Ground. The Rec, as it was usually known, was at the end of our road, reached by crossing over a huge roundabout which was planted with colourful bedding plants in summer and various types of greenery in winter. The Rec was owned by the local council and had beautiful flower beds and borders tended by two or three enthusiastic gardeners. The smell of the hyacinths in springtime and the sight of the double row of flowering cherry trees remain with me. Sadly the iron railings had been taken away to aid the war effort. The park keeper, Mr Furr, was in charge. Every evening he locked the park gates, which seemed stupid to me as there were no railings to keep people out. He had served in the army during the First World War and was very strict, keeping everyone in order. Fortunately, he lived next door to us, so we received very special attention.

The Rec boasted a putting green and tennis courts. We sometimes had a game of putting in the fenced-off area with

Bancroft Recreation Ground.

Blakes Picturedrome, Ickleford Road.

Hermitage Road looking past Barker's woodyard to the Hermitage cinema.

The Victoria public house.

Mum and Dad on a Sunday evening, but this treat didn't happen very often as money was scarce. The tennis courts were for grown-ups, so we weren't interested; but our minds were changed as teenagers when boys arrived on the scene. There were swings and a seesaw in the play area and a large concrete pond about twelve inches deep. The pond wasn't cleaned out very often, and the concrete bottom quickly became slippery. Most days someone fell in, fully clothed, which caused both tears and laughter, depending on whether you were paddling or watching.

We played rounders and cricket in front of the pavilion during the summer holidays, our cardigans acting as posts. A huge tree was our wicket. The wear and tear took its toll on the beautifully manicured lawns, and bare patches soon appeared; but, fortunately for us, Mr Furr turned a blind eye.

The Victorian bandstand played host to local bands once a month on a Sunday evening, when we were taken to sit on

The bandstand at Bancroft Recreation Ground.

uncomfortable, rickety iron chairs. The slats of the chairs were really hard and painful and marked our small legs and bottoms through our thin summer dresses. The Salvation Army Band, the Hitchin Town Band and sometimes the band from the local RAF station took turns to entertain us, all splendidly attired in their uniforms. Brass bands still remind me of those warm Sunday evenings.

The pavilion was where the tennis players and bowlers changed. It always smelled musty. There was a small tea room at one end where Mum served tea and buns once a week, and we were allowed to sit inside at a table with a biscuit and a glass of lemonade.

The place that affected our lives the most was the bowling green. That was because most of Dad's spare time was spent there in the summer. It always smelled of recently cut grass. The greens were perfect – smooth and close-cut with edges clipped, straight and tidy. Flat bowling shoes had to be worn, and children were not allowed unaccompanied inside the neatly cut hedges surrounding the greens. I was allowed to sit on a bench when Mum went to watch, but this was not very often – she would rather Dad had stayed at home.

"Do you have to play so often?" she would ask, but she knew that there was no point waiting for an answer.

I can still hear the men's voices as each bowl was released and rolled slowly and smoothly across the greens. There were very few ladies playing – equality had scarcely arrived in Hitchin.

"Bit longer, George – just a few inches short."

"Lovely one, Henry."

"A bit wide, Jim."

Arms would wave and signals known only to the players would be given. The click of the bowls knocking together, as they were moved once each end was finished, had a special noise. Dad won many trophies and was a county player.

I remember Butts Close, a large field which is said to be

Dad, my great grandmother and aunts outside the Old Bull's Head.

Hitchin's oldest open space, next to the swimming pool in Fishponds Road. Dad told me that archery practice used to take place there – hence the name – and, in the past, townspeople were entitled to graze their cattle there at certain times of the year. I remember it as the place where the circus pitched its big top and the fairground sprang up overnight once a year.

There were two cinemas in Hitchin and, as small children, for a special treat Mum and Dad would take us either to the Regal or The Hermitage. The seats cost one and sixpence for adults and nine pence for children, so we didn't go very often. As teenagers, Saturday night meant going to the pictures. Rain or shine we would queue for an hour in the company of boys and girls from our school. Sometimes we had a special boyfriend, and we would rush to get a seat in the back row of the balcony; but as we were only thirteen or fourteen years old these boyfriends evaporated when we left school.

We often visited the cattle market in Payne's Park, where animals of all descriptions were brought every Tuesday to be sold. Cows, sheep, pigs, chickens and rabbits – all were kept in iron pens or cages, and the auctioneer would shout out loud trying to get the best price for each animal. Then, when an acceptable price was reached, he would slap a label on the animal's back or on the cage. The smell would remind us of the country, but we could never understand the language of the auctioneer.

When I return to Hitchin I feel sad that so many of the buildings that were important to me as a child have disappeared. Nightingale Road and Brand Street Methodist chapels, where I spent many happy hours, have long since been flattened – as has the Old Hale Way school, which is now a modern housing estate. Spurr's, the large department store, Barker's woodyard, Bowman's Mill, the old post office in Brand Street and the Regal and Hermitage cinemas are no more. The bacon factory in

Nightingale Road, where Mum bought bacon pieces for our bacon 'roly-poly', is just a distant memory. These were all buildings of character and have happy memories for my sister, friends and me.

As I read about its history, Hitchin is proving to have many wonderful secrets hidden away in its pages. I remember Hitchin as a pleasant market town of cobbled streets and Tudor-fronted buildings. Progress, in my opinion, has not added to its charm.

The Corn Exchange, once the British Restaurant.

Making Ends Meet

"Hurry up and get your buckets, you two. Here's the salt – put plenty in."

Jean and I looked at one another, pulling faces.

"Do we have to, Dad? You know we don't like the job. It's messy and horrible."

It was the worst job ever, but we knew that we had to get on with it. The job was 'caterpillaring'. Dad grew rows of cabbages and Brussels sprouts, and they were alive with caterpillars. They were green and brown, wrinkly and slimy. They covered the leaves and made the rows look alive as they chomped along each cabbage and Brussels-sprout plant. Our job was to pick off each horrible invader and drop it into a bucket of salty water. Once deposited they would squirm and wriggle until finally they entered the caterpillar heaven in the sky. Some of the slimy things would squash between our fingers, making them green and wet.

"Don't be such babies. Just get on with it, and I'll check the plants when I get home from work."

Dad put on his bicycle clips. We both knew that the white butterfly laid the eggs which would eventually turn into caterpillars. How could such a beautiful insect turn into something so disgusting?

"Can't we have peas or beans?" I asked hopefully, knowing what the answer would be. "We don't really like cabbage or Brussels sprouts."

"Don't answer back." Dad was getting cross. "There are lots of children who would like fresh vegetables."

Jean and I looked at each other, knowing what we were both thinking: could we post the cabbage leaves and Brussels sprouts complete with slimy caterpillars to China or even Liverpool? Perhaps not.

Not all our food during the war was difficult to obtain. Although ration books were introduced in 1940 we didn't realise just what a problem it was for Mum. I can remember her taking our ration books to David Greig's, and the assistant would cut out coupons for each item. Scissors hung from a piece of string attached to her belt. Eggs, sugar, cheese and bacon were rationed. Dry goods were kept in large sacks, weighed for each customer and packed into blue paper bags.

Ration book.

Butter was stored in huge lumps and made into butter pats with wooden spatulas and a thistle emblem was marked on each pat. Cheese was cut with a wire which sliced like magic through the enormous slabs. Once a week Mum would collect the top of the milk, which was creamy, and put it in a jam jar. Jean and I would then take turns to shake it until it turned into butter. It took ages of arm-aching exercise to obtain even a small amount.

Meat was in short supply, but Mum made lots of different meals with the limited food supply that she could obtain. Stuffed sheep's hearts were one of my favourites, and so was bacon-and-onion 'roly-poly'. Each day of the week we knew exactly what we would have for dinner – it was the same every week. Sunday, roast; Monday, shepherd's pie made from leftovers served with bubble and squeak. It never altered. On Fridays we had fish and chips.

Sweets were rationed, but we thoroughly enjoyed gobstoppers and aniseed balls, which lasted for ages and coloured our mouths. Sherbet dips were also good value. Jean and I both had a small tin which Mum would fill with cocoa and sugar before we went to school, and we would eat it at playtime – dipping our wet fingers into the mixture. (Not very hygienic, but we survived!)

Milk was delivered in a milk cart pulled by a horse. Initially we collected it in a jug, but later the horse, which was stabled behind the Regal Cinema, was replaced by a milk float and milk was delivered in bottles. I still remember the cardboard milk tops – you had to push the centre in to get to the milk.

Dad loved winkles, and my job on Saturdays during the winter was to buy a mugful from the market. Then, whilst he was watching Hitchin Town playing football, I would extricate the winkles from their shells and place them in a saucer of vinegar ready for his tea, accompanied by slices of bread and butter.

Occasionally we would visit Ransom's, a factory that made

medicines. They sold raw liquorice, which we would suck, making our tongues black. We picked hips and haws from the hedgerows in the autumn and took them to Ransom's in exchange for a few pennies.

As well as food, clothes were also rationed and only available with coupons. Mum made a lot of our dresses from cut-down aunties' dresses, and as we had a good supply of aunties we had a good supply of dresses. Handkerchiefs were made from Dad's old shirts.

There were plenty of callers to our house. The rent lady called on Mondays at lunchtime, and the rent book together with the rent had to be on the table without fail. I can never remember the money being missing.

The dustman called once a week. The petrol-driven dustcarts were made of metal with sliding covers – very noisy. The rag-and-bone man was a favourite of ours. Arriving with his horse and cart, he would call out in a loud voice:

"Any old rags, bottles or bones?"

Jean and I would rush out to the barn, take down the sacks of old rags, which hung on nails, and plonk them on the cart. After peering into the sacks, the rag-and-bone man fumbled around in his filthy coat pocket and we would wait anxiously, hoping for a reward.

"Here you are," he would say, as he placed a couple of pennies into our hands from his dirty rough one. "Don't spend it all at once."

We were always intrigued by the knife-grinder, who arrived in our street on his old bike.

"Knives to grind! Scissors to mend!" he would call out. "Bring out your knives or scissors."

Propping up the back wheel of his bike, the knife or scissors would be held against the grinding stone. Bright sparks flew in all directions as he pedalled away, turning the stone which was attached to the bicycle wheel.

Coal was rationed and delivered twice a year by horse and cart. The coalman, his eyes popping out from his black face, wore a leather tabard on which rested the heavy sacks of coal. When our coal stock was low Dad would gather up the coal dust, mix it with cement and water and make briquettes, which burnt quite well.

Waste paper, silver paper and bones were collected regularly, as were the pig bins, where any waste food was deposited. We would regularly have a table on the pavement in front of our house selling unwanted items and sometimes a few cakes made by Mum. The money went to the Red Cross. We would also knit scarves, socks and gloves for the soldiers.

We were given time off from school to go potato-picking. Clothed in a pair of Dad's old trousers tied up with string, I would climb into the farm lorry and off we would go to an outlying farm.

Dad in his beloved garden.

It was exciting to travel the few miles away from our hometown, but the work was back-breaking and dirty. At weekends during the summer holidays, pea-picking earned us a few shillings, and we would cycle to a nearby village before completing a hard day's work.

Looking back, I can see that life was hard for adults, but as children we didn't realise what we were missing. Life was very colourful. Wouldn't it be great to have a rag-and-bone man and a knife-grinder in our streets calling out their wares. Would it?

The Cold Place

I was four years old when I started my education at the British School. The large Victorian buildings which housed our school were in the centre of Hitchin. The floors of the classrooms were bare boards and the windows were set high up so that we couldn't waste time staring out. We sat on wooden benches – two to a desk – with built-in inkwells but no ink. We each had a small slate to write on, a stick of chalk and a tiny rubber.

I had been at school for three months when, after feeling unwell for a few days, I was diagnosed with scarlet fever. In the late 1930s this was a serious illness, and an ambulance was called to take me to hospital. Jean was quite pleased as she wasn't allowed to go to school because of the risk of spreading the infection. She was able to have a holiday. I can still remember the ambulance arriving outside our terraced house. It was a white, wooden vehicle, and I was lifted through the rear doors on a canvas stretcher.

The journey to Letchworth Isolation Hospital, some five miles away, was very noisy, bumpy and uncomfortable. I was scared. Mum wasn't allowed in the ambulance, so I was alone except for a rather unfriendly medical assistant.

On arrival at the hospital, I was carried inside. It was impossible to see where I was going; I could only stare up at the ceiling, but eventually I was lowered on to a bed. I looked around me. I was in a long room which seemed full of beds with black iron frames and white covers neatly tucked in around the occupants. Everyone was staring at me. There was a very unpleasant smell in the room. It smelled of carbolic soap and disinfectant, but I didn't know then what it was. The floor was covered with green linoleum, and I was to find out during my stay how cold it was to my bare feet.

Immediately I was surrounded by doctors and nurses. They didn't speak to me but to each other. They pointed at and prodded me, looked into my ears, nodded and shook their heads in turn.

"I want my mum," I said to one of the nurses. "Please can I see my mum?" I started to cry.

"Just you stop that nonsense," a thin, miserable-looking nurse said as she tucked the pure white sheets tightly around me.

I knew then that I couldn't escape.

"You can't have any visitors. You're ill, and visitors are not allowed into the ward because they'll be ill if they catch scarlet fever."

I started to cry again. I had never been away from my mother and I felt ill. My throat and my ears hurt. I wanted someone to cuddle me.

"Your family can visit you next Sunday," said the nurse, "but they'll have to stand on steps outside the window. They are not allowed inside."

The doctors and nurses departed and I was left alone. After what seemed like ages, a young nurse sat down next to my bed.

"Drink this," she said kindly, handing me a small glass. "It's your medicine and you must drink it all. It'll make you better."

"Can I go home, please?" I asked her. "I don't like it here. I want my mum."

The nurse held my hand.

"You'll have to stay for a little while," she said, "just until you are better."

She seemed kind – much nicer than the skinny nurse.

"What's that white thing over your mouth?" I asked. "And why are you wearing gloves?"

"It's so that I don't catch scarlet fever," she replied.

I must have looked puzzled.

"You've got scarlet fever."

"Will you look after me?" I asked her. "Please."

"Most of the time I'll be your nurse, but when I'm not working someone else will care for you. My name is Nurse Mary, by the way.

During the next few days I came to accept Mary as my only friend. I hated the days when she was off duty. The ward was full of children and young women, but I was the youngest patient. The ward was cold and bare. There were no pictures on the walls and no curtains. There were no books to look at and hardly any toys. Most of the patients were kept in bed, only allowed to get up for a short while in the afternoon once they were almost better and ready to go home.

"It's Sunday today." Nurse Mary had arrived with my breakfast. "It's Easter Sunday so your mum and dad can come and see you and bring you an Easter egg." She handed me a dish of lumpy porridge. "Eat up."

The morning seemed endless. Visitors were allowed between two and three o'clock. I still felt ill, but the thought of seeing Mum and Dad made me feel much better. Dinner was supposed to be roast beef, but it wasn't like Mum's. The vegetables were cold and soggy and the rice pudding, like the porridge, was lumpy. I decided that I would ask Mum and Dad to take me home.

I didn't know what time it was – there wasn't a clock in the ward, and in any case I couldn't tell the time. I hated being in hospital. I longed to be back home in our small house, where it was so warm and cosy. I didn't even mind sharing the big iron bed with my sister. I wanted Mum and Dad to take me home with them, away from that horrible place.

The other patients seemed to be getting excited – perhaps it was time for the visitors to arrive. I looked anxiously towards the door at the end of the ward, fidgeting with the bandages that bound my infected ears.

A knock on the window behind my bed made me jump. Peering in, my parents were waving and smiling and holding up an Easter egg. I'd forgotten that they couldn't come into the ward. I couldn't hear what they were saying – the window was closed and I couldn't hear through my bandages. I couldn't get a cuddle or a kiss – just a wave, a smile and an Easter egg. I burst into tears.

"Come along, now." Nurse Mary put her arm around my shoulder. "Don't make your mum and dad cry. They've come a long way on the bus to see you. Give them a smile."

I could see tears slowly falling down Mum's face as I struggled to smile. Behind my parents I could see Jean standing on tiptoe at the top of the ladder. Auntie Glad and Auntie May were there too. Auntie May held up another Easter egg. They hadn't forgotten me, but I knew I wouldn't get a cuddle and I wouldn't be going home.

There were to be two more Sunday visits from Mum and Dad before I was well enough to go home. I still hated being in hospital – the bare, cold and unfriendly ward seemed like a jail. During the second week of my stay I made friends with another patient, a twelve year old girl called Joan, and she helped to cheer me up when Nurse Mary was off duty.

The day finally arrived when I was to leave hospital. It had been difficult for Mum to make the arrangements as I couldn't travel on a bus. I had to be taken home by car. We didn't have a car and we didn't know anyone who did. Dad didn't have enough money for a taxi and it was too far to walk.

Granny Kitchener finally came up with the solution. Her grocer, Mr Pembleton, who owned the local corner shop, had a car which he used to deliver groceries. Gran offered him some money, and he agreed to collect me and Mum and drive us home. Mum arrived in good time on the bus and waited in the corridor outside the ward. I was very excited. I was going home and I had never ridden in a car before. Nurse Mary helped me to pack my few belongings into a carrier bag – toothbrush, flannel and spare nightie.

One of the nurses had washed my hair in readiness for my return home, and it was hanging lank and wet, dripping on my clean frock. Nurse Mary was the only person who came to say goodbye. Joan had returned home the previous day. I looked around the ward. I was never coming back. The cold, bare floor and iron bedsteads seemed to stare back at me and the closed uncurtained windows were ready for the next group of visitors to peer through.

Me, aged about five.

"Don't come back," Nurse Mary called out as I walked unsteadily through the ward towards my mother.

"I won't," I called to her. "I'm going home."

Mr Pembleton smiled as he opened the door of his car. Mum climbed inside and I sat on her lap. She gave me a cuddle. I had waited three weeks for this.

"I'm never going back there," I told her, "never ever."

"Come on – we'll soon be home," she replied. "Let's get going."

The First Siren

The winter of 1939/40 was a time of new experiences which were difficult to understand. Jean was six and I was five when war was declared. We were both too young to realise the seriousness of it all.

At first it was exciting – there were lots of people in uniform, there were gas masks to try on and silver barrage balloons overhead, but best of all we loved watching the aeroplanes flying past on their way to London and the south coast. We waved and cheered as the planes flew over. Sometimes we could even see the pilots. Then, after a few months, when nothing much had happened, we lost interest. Life continued much as before. Being at war was boring.

Winter crept up on our family in Ickleford Road. The evenings were dark and there were no friendly street lamps to guide us home. The new blackout curtains and shutters hid the warm glow of gaslights from passers-by.

"Did you see old Mrs Walker in her front room? She'd better pull her curtains or the warden will be knocking on her door."

We were all a little scared of Jim, our air-raid warden, and his shouts of "Put that light out!"

Jean and I always went to bed at seven o'clock.

"Come on, now – it's bedtime. Up those apples and pears both of you."

Dad was strict about bedtime, and seven o'clock was his deadline.

There was no electricity in our small terraced house, so Mum carefully carried a night light up the steep stairs to our bedroom. The flame reflected on the brass stair rods – all thirteen of them. I knew that there were thirteen, as we had to clean them every Saturday morning. We would tip the Brasso out of the blue-and-red-striped tin into the flat lid. It has a smell of its own – difficult to describe. There would be icicles inside our bedroom window by morning. The flame of the night light flickered – the smell of wax wafted up the narrow staircase. There was nowhere for it to escape to.

The linoleum on the floor of our bedroom was cold to our feet so in winter we undressed downstairs in front of the fire.

"Quick – jump into bed. Snuggle down underneath the eiderdown. I want no noise. Understand?"

We jumped into bed. We had two hot-water bottles: a rubber one, soft and cuddly like a teddy bear, and a stone bottle, too hot to touch. We took it in turns with the bottles, and that night it was Jean's turn with the rubber one.

'Lucky her!' I thought.

Then we stiffened as the dreaded siren sounded – the first siren of the war. It was loud, wailing, terrifying. We lay like statues in our bed, too scared to move. Our mouths were dry with fear. We clung together, crying softly so Mum didn't hear us.

Were we going to die?

We knew that Mum was alone downstairs as Dad had gone down to the warden's shelter at the end of Periwinkle Lane. He was head warden and spent a great deal of time in the damp, cold, dungeon-like shelter, built underground and reached by eight steep concrete steps. I could picture him puffing on his Woodbines. The wardens patrolled the streets – checking for lights. They were the men who set off the sirens when news of approaching enemy planes was telephoned through.

"Mum! Mum!" we both screamed out.

We tried to comfort each other as we heard the living-room door open. Mum appeared in the bedroom doorway, candle in one hand, shielding the flame with the other.

"Come on, you two – downstairs." Mum was a woman of few words. "Stop that noise and put your dressing gowns on."

Jean clung to me.

"Don't go without me. Wait."

Swiftly we jumped out of bed and followed Mum downstairs, pulling our dressing gowns around our shoulders. This was our first air raid, and we didn't know what to do. No one had told us what to expect. Would the Germans drop their bombs on our house?

The siren stopped; the wailing finished. Now there was only silence.

"In you go."

Mum gave us a gentle push, and we found ourselves inside the cupboard under the stairs. This was our makeshift shelter – thought to be the safest place in the house until the promised Anderson shelter arrived.

The cupboard was our larder. It was the place where we kept our food, stored in packets and tins on wooden shelves which ran the length of the cupboard. Here was stored newly

Anderson shelter

51

baked bread, Camp coffee and cakes. There were jars of jam, pickles, rice, sugar and tea. A dish of Brussels sprouts, left over from dinner, filled the air with the horrible smell that only sprouts can give out. They would be joined later by cold potatoes to make Dad's favourite supper of 'bubble and squeak'. Even now I cannot cook that dish without remembering those early days of the war.

We lay down on a mat on the floor and covered ourselves with a blanket, clinging to each other for comfort. A small torch was our only light, and we moved it around the tiny place of safety, shining it on the underside of the stairs just above our heads, making shadows of varying shapes and sizes. It was a tight squeeze, and we found ourselves kicking each other as we fought for space in which to stretch our legs.

"Move your feet!" Jean shouted. "I haven't got enough room."

"Neither have I," I replied. "Give me some room as well."

We drew apart. The closeness of our bodies and lack of space made us forget the siren for a few minutes.

"Keep quiet, you two, and try and get some sleep."

Mum was busy ironing. I could hear her lift the flat iron from the kitchen range and the hiss as she spat on the bottom of the iron to test the heat. It was impossible to sleep – we were too scared and we didn't like being in this tiny space.

"Let's play I spy."

Jean was trying to be brave.

"You can't see enough with a torch," I replied, "so stop being so silly."

Jean sat up, stretching her arm towards the shelf holding the biscuit tin, and suddenly a loud noise broke the silence. We clung to each other.

"What was that?" Jean cried out.

"Thunder – it was thunder." I didn't know what else to say. "Let's snuggle down and get to sleep."

Jean, our evacuee and me.

The cupboard door opened wide and Mum popped her head into the dark space.

"Are you both all right?" she asked. "Would you like a drink of milk and a biscuit?"

"What was that noise, Mum?" I asked. "We're scared."

"Nothing to worry about," she told us. "The all-clear will go soon, and then you can go back to bed."

I looked at Mum's face. I could see that she was scared as well.

Eventually the welcome noise of the all-clear sounded. The danger was over – well, for tonight anyway.

"Come on, you two – back to bed and no noise!" Mum was her old self again. "Hurry up and get to sleep – you've got school tomorrow."

We snuggled down in our large, comfortable bed. Jean wanted a glass of water, but she was too scared to go downstairs. Slowly I crept out of the bedroom and down the stairs, trying to pluck up enough courage to open the door to the living room. The scullery door banged shut. Dad had returned from the shelter.

"You OK, Lil?"

I heard Dad put his tin hat down on the table.

"Yes, we're OK, but the kids were scared. Was the explosion close?"

"They were aiming for the railway lines, but they didn't hit them, luckily. What's for supper?"

I crept slowly back to our bedroom – Jean would have to manage without a drink. We had survived our first air raid and we were safe.

Educating Molly

School for Jean and me was two very different experiences: I really enjoyed learning, whilst Jean enjoyed going to school but not learning.

Because Jean and I were both born in the same calendar year, we were both in the same class. This wouldn't happen today, and it did cause many problems. We started at our first school – the British School – when we were four years old.

The school was about a mile from our home, and we did the journey four times a day. There were no school dinners, so everyone went home at midday. Mum accompanied us on these journeys and then returned to prepare dinner for us and Dad – always a hot meal (meat and two veg and a pudding). I don't know how she coped.

The British School is now a public museum. Children from local schools visit in groups dressed in Victorian costume in order to experience the Victorian way of education.

"Sit up straight," the teacher calls out. "Hands on heads. No talking."

I remember it well. At four years of age it was very painful to sit for ages with our hands on our heads, or our hands clasped tightly behind our backs.

"Hold out your hand!"

The ruler hurt as it cut into the culprit's hand.

"Ouch!"

"Here's another one for complaining."

The boys usually got into trouble because of their fidgeting and talking.

"Jonnie, stand in the corner."

We always enjoyed Jonnie's stay in the corner – he would make faces when the teacher's back was turned.

Because the school was situated in the centre of Hitchin there was limited space outside. A small tarmacked playground was reached from our first-floor classroom by iron outside stairs. There must have been a stairway inside, but I cannot remember it.

Jean and I, with our husbands, visited the school about five years ago and were shown into a classroom full of local children dressed in Victorian costume. The teacher called the children to order.

"These two ladies were pupils here a long time ago when they were children, so you can ask them questions."

Jean and I felt about a hundred years old as the questions flowed.

"Did you use a slate?"

"What did you wear?"

"Did you ever get the cane?"

"Did you have to use outside toilets?"

The answer to most of their questions was "Yes", and we were stared at with awe and admiration.

In 1940, when schools were reorganised, we moved from the British School to Wilshere-Dacre School. Built in 1929, this was much nearer to our home, so there was not so far to walk. In those days it seemed to us that Wilshere-Dacre School existed solely to prepare pupils for the entrance examination for the local grammar schools. There were two classes in each year – the A and B classes. If you were unfortunate enough to be allocated a place in the B class, you had little chance of being entered for the examination. Jean and I were both in the A class, so we had some expectations. Each class was divided into four rows – the brightest in row one, and so on. Needless to say, the pupils in row one were certainties for grammar-school places.

The school had very high standards, in both educational matters and school uniforms, which were navy with a yellow stripe around the neck.

"Come to the front, everyone who has a school uniform," the headmaster would call out at assembly.

All the children who were lucky enough to have school uniforms – mostly from the top groups – would assemble smugly in front of the rest of the school. Jean and I had uniforms, but if our jumpers were in the wash we couldn't wear them. I recall going to the front of assembly on such a day only to be sent back.

"You're not wearing the proper jumper," I was told.

"But you said all pupils who have a school uniform come to the front."

I still remember how angry I felt, and I could only have been eight or nine years old.

Lessons were taken up a notch or two the year before the dreaded entrance examination took place. My parents then decided that Jean and I were not to be entered. The reason given was that they couldn't afford the uniforms or equipment needed. I think, in retrospect, the real reason was because they thought that there might be problems if one of us passed and the other failed. I have often wondered just how difficult this decision was for them, but it was a decision that would change my life.

Because we were not entered for the grammar-school examination, when I was ten and Jean eleven we transferred to the secondary modern school in Old Hale Way, which we thought sounded rather grand. The school, now demolished to make way for modern houses, was built just before the Second World War broke out. It boasted two wings – one for girls and the other for boys – joined at the front by a large kitchen and at the back by a shared gymnasium. Boys and girls had separate entrances and were not allowed to mix. A large playing field ran along the back of the school, and there was a white line dividing the boys' space from the girls'. The field along the line was muddy and bare, but no one dared to cross it. The edge of the playing field bordered a field of wheat, so it felt like being in the middle of the country.

I recall my first day at the Old Hale Way school. We rose early, Jean and I, and washed in the cold scullery. Then we struggled into our new school uniforms, consisting of a white blouse and navy gymslip, a navy jumper with a blue stripe around the neck, and a blue and grey tie. I had never worn a tie before, and it was difficult to tie the knot, but eventually it met with Dad's approval. Navy knickers were compulsory, but they felt uncomfortable – hard and itchy. The pocket housing my handkerchief made an embarrassing bulge.

A quick breakfast of porridge and we were ready! Jean was not eager – she dawdled just to annoy me. Slowly and reluctantly she pulled on her new gabardine raincoat.

"Got your dinner money?" Mum was fussing.

I nodded. I had tucked two shillings, which was a week's dinner money, safely in my new brown leather satchel, which had my name inside. It also held a brand-new exercise book, and a pencil and rubber tucked inside my silver wooden pencil box.

"Come on, Jean – we'll be late."

I wheeled my new bike out of the barn and set off down the passageway. I was so proud of this bike, bought for £9 from Wiggs Cycle Shop in Bancroft. It was black all over. All bikes in 1943 were black, owing to a shortage of paint, but I didn't mind. We left our bikes in the bike shed and entered the school. It seemed enormous after our junior school.

We were all marched into the hall for assembly. The headmistress, Miss Gunn, and the other teachers sat in a semicircle on chairs on the raised platform. The new girls sat cross-legged on the floor at the front. Spaced around the hall were older girls sitting on chairs, and at the front was a tall girl I later learned was called Mary.

"She's head girl," Audrey, my best friend, told me in a whisper, "and the others are prefects."

I hadn't a clue what a prefect was or what a head girl did, but I knew that I would rather sit on a chair than on the floor. I decided there and then that if I couldn't go to the grammar school, I would be head girl. I don't think it was only because of the seating arrangements. Four years later, as the headmistress pinned the head girl's badge to my jumper, I felt that this was my first real achievement.

The PE teacher scared me at first. She always wore perfectly ironed pleated shorts. She was very strict and expected everyone to obey her instructions without question. The gym was huge. Ropes hung from the ceiling, and there were lots of pieces of apparatus stacked around the walls. I loved PE and games, and I was sure that the teacher wouldn't be too bad when I got used to her. After PE we all had to take a shower. I'd never had a shower before – we didn't even have a bathroom at home. It was lovely. There was lots of hot water – as much as we wanted.

Dinner was eaten in the hall. It was delicious. On the first day it was macaroni cheese and tapioca pudding with jam. We had a glass of water each and said grace before we were allowed to sit down. The teacher on dinner duty was the PE teacher, and she spent most of the dinner hour pulling girls' shoulders back. She would put one of her knees in the middle of the unfortunate girl's back and say loudly, "Sit up straight."

We soon learned to sit up before she reached our table.

After dinner, the hardest task for most girls was writing out the timetable without making a blot. This sheet of precious paper had to last all year. The timetable gave us an insight into the joys we could expect in the next four years, including unfamiliar subjects like mathematics, science, geography and history. Our education was to be broadened beyond our wildest dreams.

We were divided into houses named after Commonwealth countries – Canada, South Africa, Australia and India. Jean and I were in India. Marks for excellence were added to India's

The gym at the Old Hale Way school.

The British School.

School camp.

Wilshere-Dacre School.

total, and 'order' marks were subtracted. 'It's a pity Jean is in India,' I thought. 'She will collect order marks by the bucketful.'

Sadly, at 3.30 the first day at our new school was over. We packed away our school books and filled our satchels with brand-new exercise books which would eventually contain our homework.

"Don't forget to bring twopence for the school fund tomorrow," our form teacher shouted above the noise of banging desk lids. "And stop talking in the classroom."

I remember this as a good school. The lessons were varied, but obviously they had their limitations. As well as the usual lessons, we learned how to sew and cook, and we did shorthand and typing and pottery. We even learned how to grow vegetables in the school garden. We had a wonderful English teacher, and she introduced me to Shakespeare, poetry and Rudyard Kipling. I can still recite all the verses of 'The Glory of the Garden'. She produced very professional school plays at Christmas, and in the art room we made our own scenery and painted costumes. There were no examinations to pass or qualifications to obtain, but the teachers did their best to make school interesting. Eventually the PE teacher was replaced by a very young and pretty lady with blonde hair and blue eyes. Most of us had a crush on her, and several of us even attended her wedding at Letchworth as uninvited guests.

The girls in the fourth year made the school-uniform dresses for the first-year pupils; so, as you can imagine, the standard of most was not too high, and because it was wartime the material was of poor quality. In the first year, ten- and eleven-year-olds made their own cookery caps and aprons. This was a very good experience, and I was able to 'dress-make' from a very early age.

In the third year we worked for our county badge. We chose a subject for a project, which could be on anything we wanted. I chose 'Farming Through the Ages' as I had dreams of marrying a farmer and this would come in useful. I wrote to a firm called

Trusty Tractors asking for their brochure. Imagine my horror when as well as receiving their literature they sent me an appointment with one of their salesmen. They told me he would bring a tractor along to my home to give me a demonstration. I was scared. We lived in a terraced house, and its back garden was reached through a narrow passageway. It was certainly not suitable for a large tractor. Dad hurried to the nearest public telephone box to telephone Trusty Tractors, and, much to my relief, he was able to cancel the appointment.

As well as our project we had to complete various tasks in the gymnasium and the local swimming pool. With my long legs I was a natural in the high jump and hurdles. We also went out on a day's hike in the Hertfordshire countryside using a map and compass. It was all very good training for later life.

One evening, after completing our day's expedition, Jean and I took turns to have a strip wash in the scullery whilst Dad mended a pair of shoes on the table next to us. A knock on the door made us jump. Imagine our surprise and embarrassment when Dad opened the door to find our headmistress. She had come to ask whether we had returned home safely. She was a very caring lady, and I still have fond memories of her.

We were eventually taken by coach to County Hall in Hertford and presented with our county badges. It was a memorable experience.

After four years at secondary school there was nowhere else to go except the workplace. There were courses for nursing and catering cadets, but neither of these appealed to me. The school leaving age had been raised to fifteen, and I had one extra term before my fifteenth birthday and my first job in the real world.

My Sunday-school teacher knew of a chiropodist who needed a receptionist, and I went along to her surgery on several Saturdays so that she could see whether I was suitable. I worked eight hours a day with no pay and really enjoyed the work. She promised to teach me how to mix the creams and help with the patients, so I was really excited. The day before I was due to leave school I received a letter from her saying that she had decided not to have a receptionist, so there wasn't a job for me.

Welcome to the real world!

The last day of term – leaving day – was a day of excitement and sadness. As head girl it was my job to present the headmistress, Miss Gunn, with flowers and thank both her and the other teachers for their hard work. I cycled into town and bought the flowers, balancing them in my bike basket for the journey back to school.

The school was assembled in the hall. We sang the school hymn – 'I Vow to Thee, My Country'. Prayers were said and Miss Gunn wished the leavers good luck. Now it was my turn. Trembling, I climbed the steps to the stage, flowers clutched tightly in my hand. I thanked the teachers and gave Miss Gunn the flowers.

"Three cheers for Miss Gunn – hip hip hooray! Three cheers for the teachers – hip hip hooray! Three cheers for the school – hip hip hooray!"

The cheers died away and the girls filed out of the hall. A part of my life was ending. I was leaving my happy schooldays behind. Next day I must go to the labour exchange and find a job.

'What does the future hold?' I wondered.

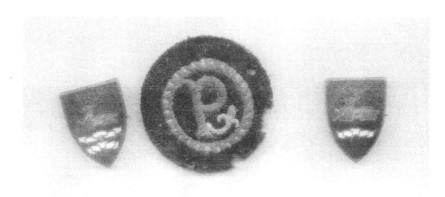

Prefect and county badges.

An Unforgettable Character

I always remember Mr Furr as being an old man, but he could only have been about fifty when I was a child. He lived next door to us with his wife and their unmarried daughter, Kitty.

He was the park keeper of Bancroft Recreation Ground in Hitchin, and he always carried a walking cane with a gold knob at the end. He walked erect, like a soldier. I expect this was the result of the years he spent serving in the army during the First World War. His waxed moustache and deep, piercing blue eyes added to the picture of someone in control. I can see him now with his gold watch and chain, which he frequently took out of his waistcoat pocket, snapping open the cover, checking the time and swiftly tucking it away again.

If ever I or my friends were in trouble with older boys whilst playing in the Rec, Mr Furr would stride over to us and scold the boys, gathering us about him. He would wave his cane in the air to threaten them, but I never saw him use it. We really felt safe in his presence and considered him our personal bodyguard.

Mr Furr's duties at Bancroft Recreation Ground were many and varied. Apart from making sure that the children were behaving properly and were safe, he supervised the tennis courts and putting greens and kept a wary eye out for vandals, who frequently damaged the beautiful flowerbeds or trespassed in the bandstand. He also patrolled the bowling greens, which,

Gardening at Ickleford Road.

with their Cumberland turf, looked like velvet. The greens were mown almost every day, and, needless to say, they were out of bounds to children. Mr Furr would sometimes allow me to sit quietly on one of the uncomfortable green-painted iron seats around the edge of the greens when my father was playing bowls.

At home Mr Furr was a different person – no longer stern and upright, but gentle, kind and clever with his hands. He always called me Mistress Molly, which made me feel special – almost royal – and because he was the only person to afford me this title, he became my special friend. I followed him about like a young puppy.

Often, when I wasn't at school, I would finish my jobs for Mum and make my way to Mr Furr's large wooden shed at the top of his garden. I was always made to feel welcome.

"Hello, Mistress Molly. Come in. I need some help today."

A wooden bench took up one side of the shed, and numerous shelves stacked high with jars and rusty tins filled the other. Two battered wooden chairs were tucked under the bench. He always mended his own and his family's shoes as money was scarce, and the shed smelled of leather and leather dye. Before escaping to his beloved garden shed, he would change from his working clothes into a pair of old baggy trousers and a worn jumper. It was fascinating to watch him. Puffing away at his old pipe, which he relit frequently, first he would cut the leather to a rough shape and nail it to the shoe, which would be sitting on the iron last.

"Be careful!" I would say. "Don't cut your fingers."

I was always scared that he would cut himself as he trimmed away the leather with a very sharp knife and then tidied up the edges with a file, but he never did. His gnarled brown hands worked swiftly as he painted the edges with dye. As soon as the shoes were dry, he would give them a quick polish and the job would be complete.

"That's another pair finished," he would say as he gathered

up his tools and put everything away tidily. "Mother will be pleased."

"What are we going to do next?" I would ask him. "Can we do some gardening, please? You promised to show me how to grow flowers. You know that Dad only grows vegetables."

Mr Furr was a skilled gardener and a patient teacher. My father was an enthusiastic gardener, growing magnificent vegetables and fruit, but Mr Furr's garden was full of exciting plants, which made a patchwork of colour. In the summer this patch of garden was perfumed by a row of sweet peas. These beautiful, delicate flowers seemed to bloom for weeks on end. He taught me how to grow large chrysanthemums by removing the small buds; how to make new plants by taking cuttings; and how to grow flowers from seed. He could also turn a pink hydrangea blue by adding a magic powder. Nothing, it seemed, was too difficult for him to cope with. We would spend hours together in his garden, and to me it was fascinating and absorbing. Nothing was too much trouble, and the hours flew by when I was in his company.

The apple tree next to the shed was full of pink blossom in the spring, and in the autumn it was weighed down by fruit – lovely, sharp-tasting, crisp apples.

"Shall we try one of these apples? Do you think they are ready to pick?"

He would pick one from the tree and cut it into slices with his penknife.

"What do you think about that – is it ripe enough?"

We would happily bite into it, the juice running down our chins. We never told anyone that we picked the apples. This was our secret. Under the apple tree there was a small patch of lily of the valley. In the spring the heavy scent mixed with the strong smell of the newly turned soil – brown and moist, waiting for its seeds and tubers; waiting for its chance to produce its abundant harvest.

Mr Furr's shed was, as I have said, at the very end of the garden, and our silence would be broken at mealtimes by Mrs Furr blowing a whistle. This meant that dinner or tea was ready and Mr Furr had to hurry to the house and prepare himself for his meal. I always knew what his next words would be:

"I must go now – time for dinner. I mustn't keep Mother waiting."

Sadly, Mrs Furr had to be obeyed. I grew to hate that whistle, as it meant an end to our time together. Mrs Furr was a tiny lady but the power of that whistle was overwhelming, and Mr Furr had to go. The shed would be locked, and with a final look at the plants we would trudge hand in hand down the garden path.

Gardening at Ickleford Road.

Mr Furr's expertise extended to mending clocks and watches. His most treasured possession was a beautiful grandfather clock, which stood grandly in the corner of his small front room. The clock chimed every quarter of an hour, and I always wondered how it worked. In the winter, I was occasionally invited into this room to sit cross-legged in front of my old friend next to his musical clock. He would take a key out of his sideboard drawer and put it one at a time into the three keyholes on the clock's face, turning it slowly and deliberately. The clock would then start to chime and the tick-tock seemed much louder.

Old Mr Furr was the perfect friend for me, always ready to help me out of trouble and to teach me how to make my life more enjoyable. When he died I felt that no one could take his place. Now I know that he will always be part of my life as he gave me an introduction to my favourite pastime – gardening. He will always be in my thoughts.

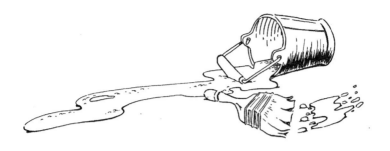

When Father Papered the Parlour

I was twelve in the spring of 1945. Everyone was looking forward to a life of peace and prosperity, but in reality we still had to endure rationing and shortages.

It was during this period that Dad decided to decorate our living room. The room was small – probably about ten foot by ten – and it was the hub of our small Victorian terraced house. We ate in it and played in it. We did our homework on the wooden table (scrubbed by Mum every Friday) and relaxed, listening to the wireless which stood on the bamboo table in the corner of the room.

The room was badly in need of attention. The ceiling, once white, was a mottled brown, stained by smoke from the old range (now replaced with a modern tiled fireplace) and Dad's Woodbines. The pink floral wallpaper was faded, and where the wall met the ceiling it was hanging off in places. In the corners of the room Jean had poked her fingers through, making a series of holes.

The room was cleared in readiness for redecorating. The ottoman, where my sister and I would lie recovering from measles, chickenpox or various other childhood illnesses, had been moved into the front room, as had the pictures, mirror and chairs. The rag rugs had been rolled up and the curtains taken down. The room looked sad and unloved. When Granny Foster arrived some years earlier to live with us she brought with her a beautiful sideboard, which stood in the living room, but after a row with Mum she had departed to her son's home in Welwyn Garden City taking it with her.

Dad decided that I was to be his helper – probably because I was taller than Jean and more likely to be useful when it came to papering the ceiling. My father was short (about five feet four inches tall), so he needed someone with long legs and arms. The job was to be completed in one day as Dad had to be at work the following day.

We started early, Dad standing on a pair of rickety wooden steps whilst I balanced on a wooden box borrowed from the local greengrocer. We stripped the paper from the walls and ceiling, packing it into a pair of hessian sacks. It was a dirty job and hard work, and the room looked even more unloved than it did before we started. The walls were uneven – full of small holes where the plaster came away with the wallpaper. I hoped Dad would be able to fill them before the distemper was applied.

A wonderful smell came from the scullery next door, where Mum and Jean were preparing dinner. Dinner was usually eaten at twelve thirty, but if Dad was on nights it could be delayed for up to an hour so that he could get a few hours' sleep. I didn't like it when Dad was on nights as we had to be quiet so as not to wake him.

Dinner that day was bacon-and-onion roll, followed by jam roly-poly and custard. Mum would roll the suet crust pastry out, place the bacon and onion at one end and the raspberry jam at the other. Then she would roll it up carefully and twist the middle so that the bacon and jam didn't meet. The pudding was then wrapped in a piece of old sheet and placed in a large saucepan of boiling water, where it bubbled away all morning, reminding us of the joys to come.

Dad unrolled the ceiling paper, having mixed a bucketful of paste which resembled vomit. It glistened in the white enamel bucket and stuck to the brushes. He didn't feel the need to measure the ceiling – he just held the paper against the wall and cut it. If it was too long, he snipped the end off; if it was too short, he would utter a few words which I wasn't supposed to hear and let a piece in. Now came the difficult part – sticking the paper to the ceiling. He pasted the paper on the table, which I had helpfully covered with the *News of the World*, but both the ceiling paper and the newspaper ended up screwed up and thrown on the floor accompanied by a few well-chosen very rude words. The newsprint had come off on to the ceiling paper. Well, I didn't know much about decorating. He cut another piece of paper, pasted it, folded it neatly and handed it to me to hold. I had borrowed an old shirt of Dad's to protect my own clothes, and Dad wore his old paint-spattered shirt and trousers. We looked a scruffy pair.

I walked over to the ladder, where Dad was perched, and handed him the sticky paper. He took it carefully and patted it into place. I took the other end of the roll to the far end of the room and stood on my box, holding it above my head. Dad descended the ladder and climbed on to the box beside me, but as he stuck my end of the paper to the ceiling the other end fell down, wrapping itself around his head and shoulders. Trying hard not to laugh, I closed my ears to his expected outburst.

"Hold the bloody paper up! Don't let your end fall down! Look what you're doing!"

It was going to be a long day.

Dad wrestled with the paper, removing it from his hair and clothes. I held on to my end, not daring to move. My arms, neck and shoulders felt numb. I wondered how long I could survive, relieved that it was such a small room. It took the rest of the morning to paper the ceiling. Both Dad and I were repeatedly covered in sticky, wet ceiling paper, and I had to endure his bad language and foul temper.

Dinner gave us a welcome break. We ate it in the front room,

Dad with his bowls trophy.

which was a real treat as we were usually allowed in the room only on special occasions. The black leather settee and chairs were cold and uncomfortable, but we were able to gaze at the two enormous pictures which almost covered the tiny walls.

"Come on – let's get going. We'll never get it done if you sit here dreaming all day."

Slowly I joined Dad in the living room. I wasn't feeling enthusiastic and I had eaten too much. The afternoon was to be taken up with distempering the walls. It was impossible to buy wallpaper so we couldn't hide the uneven walls under the cover of pink roses. Dad didn't feel the need to fill in the holes, so the distemper would have to do.

'What colour will it be?' I wondered, hoping for something in a pastel shade.

Dad had bought the only tin of distemper available in Woolworth's and he wasn't sure of the colour. He took a screwdriver and prised off the lid. I took a deep breath. It was the most awful shade of dark greeny-blue. It was horrible. What would Mum think?

"That looks nice," Dad said: "a nice change from pink."

I nodded miserably, taking the large brush and dipping it into the mixture. 'Perhaps it will dry a paler shade,' I prayed.

All afternoon we worked, mostly in silence, painting over the uneven walls. Fortunately the ceiling paper remained in place. I couldn't have coped with any more bad language.

At last it was finished and Dad stepped down from his ladder. I scrambled down from my wooden box and we stood back to examine our handiwork.

"Looks good, doesn't it?" Dad looked at me for my approval. "Nice colour!" he added. "Put your brush in the jam jar and we'll get cleaned up."

The sun shone in through the casement window, showing up the uneven walls, but Dad didn't seem to notice. He had decorated the room as he said he would, and that was that.

The door opened and Mum and Jean walked in. I held my breath.

"That looks nice, dear," said Mum. "Lovely colour!"

Jean looked at me and winked. "Lovely colour!" she said. "Really nice!"

We all set to and cleaned up the mess. Mum scrubbed the linoleum and the furniture; the pictures and mirror were replaced; clean curtains were hung. Soon everything was back to normal. Dad and Mum were smiling and the sun was shining. We ate tea at six o'clock – watercress sandwiches and plain cake with jam.

"You're excused washing-up," Dad told me. "You've worked really hard today. Just one more thing to do."

My heart sank. 'No more decorating, please!' I prayed. My body was exhausted.

"Get washed. We're going out, you and me."

Slowly I walked into the scullery and drew a bowl of cold water. I couldn't wash my sticky hair as it was Monday and hair-washing only took place in the tin bath on Fridays. I cleaned myself as best I could and put on a clean frock.

"Come on, my girl." Dad opened the scullery door and we walked out into the garden. "You and I are going to the circus."

Hand in hand we walked along the road towards the field where a flag above the big top was blowing in the breeze. Dad was the best, I decided, forgetting all that had happened earlier – the bad language and evil temper – the best Dad in the entire world!

Happiness Is Sunday Tea

'All things bright and beautiful, all creatures great and small.'

The last chorus of the children's favourite hymn came to a close. The children in the Sunday-school class shuffled impatiently as the teacher said a final prayer.

"Hands together, eyes closed."

I knew that Trevor would be peeping through his fingers, hoping the teacher wouldn't see.

"You can go now."

Miss Adkins, top teacher in the primary and junior department at Nightingale Road Methodist Chapel, closed her hymn book and replaced her horn-rimmed glasses in their case. The children – all aged between three and eleven – struggled into their winter coats and pulled on their multicoloured hats, scarves and gloves. It was freezing cold and they knew the walk home would be far from pleasant.

The tiny room where the primary schoolchildren met was heated by a coke fire, which spat out black smoke and fumes. We were always glad when summer arrived and the fire remained unlit. The larger schoolroom had been taken over by airmen and was used as their billet for the duration of the war. Sometimes one or two of them would join our class and teach us a new hymn or song. We all looked forward to this treat – it was better than listening to our elderly teacher. One of the songs that a young airman taught us was:

I'm H-A-P-P-Y, I'm H-A-P-P-Y.
I know I am, I'm sure I am, I'm H-A-P-P-Y.

We all sang along with great enthusiasm, but it wasn't until years later that the penny dropped and I realised that we had been telling each other that we were happy. I laugh every time I remember.

My sister and I didn't go home after Sunday school – we always went to tea at Gran's. Auntie May and Auntie Glad, who were Sunday-school teachers at Nightingale Road Methodist Chapel, collected us, and we would start on our long walk to Gran's house in Stevenage Road, not far from the Great North Road. It was a long walk for us. We would have our hands clasped tightly by our middle-aged spinster aunts, and dawdling was not allowed. The windows of the shops in Bancroft and the High Street were dark – the shutters were pulled down. Shops didn't open on Sundays, and we were not allowed to peep through the tiny cracks around the doors. A sharp tug on our tiny arms kept us marching on.

"Come on, now! Come on!" Auntie Glad would urge us on. "Get a move on."

The worst part of the walk to Gran's was up Hitchin Hill. A wood – dark and forbidding – skirted the pavement. The iron railings had been taken away to be used for munitions, and the mud from beneath the trees had crept across the uneven path, making it slippery in both wet and icy weather.

At last, we would reach Gran's house – a middle-of-terrace house with a flat roof. Mum and Dad would be there already. Granddad would be standing at the front gate with his dog, Cody – a yappy white and brown terrier that never left his side. Granddad never spoke to us – we felt invisible in his presence.

Gran's house – it was never Granddad's – was small, but it gave shelter to Gran and Granddad and four maiden aunts: Glad, May, Gwen and Queenie. Gwen and Queenie worked

Jean and me with Auntie May.

Jean and me with Mum and Auntie Glad.

at the Spirella factory at Letchworth, and May and Glad were cleaners at the local council offices. The tiny living room was almost filled by an enormous table, a sideboard and a piano. A large black range took up one wall, and there was always a kettle boiling on the top. Around the shelf, above the range, was a white lace hanging (I'm not sure what it was called), and on the floor was a polished brass fender with a box at either end to house newspapers and wood.

The front room had been turned into a bedroom for Auntie May and Auntie Glad, but their put-you-up was folded up each morning and sometimes we were allowed to sit in there. It was in this room that Granddad lay in his coffin when Jean and I were taken in to see him and made to touch his cold, clammy forehead. We could only have been five or six years old. I can still remember how awful that felt.

Sunday tea was an important part of the week. Gran would lay the table with her best tablecloth and china, and plates of sandwiches would appear from the tiny damp scullery, carried in by the aunts. When Gran sat down, her ample figure, enveloped in an enormous floral overall tied at the back, hung over the sides of the chair. She would call out her instructions:

"Gwen, bring the jam sandwiches. May, how many paste sandwiches have you made? Glad, cut up the pork pie. Queenie, make the tea."

Mum and Dad would fuss around Jean and me, making sure we behaved ourselves. The table would gradually fill up – jellies, blancmange, cakes and biscuits – anything that could be provided from Gran's larder, bought from David Greig's with her food coupons. When it was time to sit down, I was sent to fetch Granddad, who stayed by the front gate for as long as possible. He didn't enjoy family gatherings, preferring the company of his beloved dog. I would tuck my hand into his.

"Come on, Granddad – tea's ready."

I never got an answer, but his fingers curled around mine

and I knew that we were friends. This was the best I could expect. Granddad never sat at the table with us; he always sat in his armchair by the warm range, Cody at his feet.

Tea was a busy affair – lots of passing of plates backwards and forwards – but very little conversation passed our lips. Talking at the table was forbidden. Jean and I daren't ask for food, but we had to wait until it was offered to us. After tea the table was cleared and the dishes were washed in the stone sink in the scullery, next to the mangle. Jean and I would be sent out to the lavatory in the backyard. Between the row of houses and their tiny gardens was a path connecting the back doors and lavatories of all the houses. It was always cold and dark in the dingy and smelly lavatory, so we went together and didn't linger.

Now came the most boring part of Sunday evening at Gran's: Auntie Glad and Auntie May would entertain us. May would play the out-of-tune piano (some notes didn't play at all) and sing in her wobbly voice. Glad would get out her violin to accompany her. It was awful. The screech of the violin and the missing piano notes sent Jean and me into hysterical laughter, which had to be muffled inside our handkerchiefs amid looks of dismay from Mum and Dad. At last the entertainement was over, but the worst was yet to come: the long walk home through the cold and dark. In winter it was often wet and sometimes frosty, so we would beg Dad to let us catch the bus, but there was no money for such a luxury. Tired, cold and miserable, we walked.

At last Dad would throw open our back door and herd us into the scullery.

"Here we are – home safe and sound," he would say as he rummaged in his trouser pocket for a box of matches; then he would quickly draw the blackout across the window and light the gas lamp.

Sometimes Dad would accidentally push the match through the delicate gas mantle, breaking it, and he would have to find another one quickly. We knew that the search would be accompanied by some bad language, so we kept out of his way. The fire was always out when we reached home, so the next job was to try to coax some life into it and warmth into our frozen fingers and toes.

"Time for bed!" Mum would say. "Have you enjoyed yourselves?"

"Yes, thank you," Jean and I would answer in unison, giving each other a quick nudge when Mum wasn't looking.

We would undress slowly, trying to gain some warmth from the few flames struggling in the tiny fireplace. Cold pyjamas didn't help, but Mum would boil some water on the gas stove and hand us a hot-water bottle each. The small candle, which lit our way up the narrow stairs, gave out a familiar smell and a warm glow.

The huge double bed with brass bedknobs that Jean and I shared looked welcoming, but we both knew that under the eiderdown the sheets would be freezing cold.

"School tomorrow!" Mum would say as she tucked us up. "Snuggle down and get to sleep."

We would cuddle our hot-water bottles as she blew out the candle. We shivered in unison.

'Thank goodness it won't be Sunday again for another week!' I thought. 'Let's hope Auntie Glad breaks a string on her violin and Auntie May catches a cold and has to stay in bed.'

"All things bright and beautiful . . ." I sang to myself under the covers. "I'm H-A-P-P-Y . . ."

An Afternoon Out

"Want to come out for a ride this afternoon?"

Those few words turned an ordinary day into what could only be described as a magical experience.

"Yes please, Dad."

My answer was immediate – no need to consider the offer. I could be ready to leave in two minutes flat. I rushed upstairs to the bedroom that I shared with Jean, grabbed my jumper and jumped down the steep stairs two at a time.

"I'm going out with Dad," I called to Mum, who was washing up the dinner things in the scullery. "I'll be back teatime."

"What about drying up for me before you go?"

Mum didn't turn round as I flew out of the back door.

"Be careful. Don't wander off."

I ran down the passageway to where Dad was waiting, sitting astride his bike, his trousers tucked into bicycle clips.

"I'll go and get the van and meet you in Whinbush Road," he told me.

He was off, pedalling furiously as he wobbled down the street with me running after him, trying to keep up. I made my way to Whinbush Road, and it wasn't long before the red van drew up.

My dad was a postman – not a postman who delivers letters to your door, but a 'Postman, Higher Grade', which made him seem very important to Jean and me. He worked at the Hitchin Sorting Office, which was tucked away in a side street at the back of Nightingale Road – a busy road which ran up to the railway station, past the bacon factory and Bowman's flour mill.

Dad drove a large red post-office van with lots of room in the back. His duties were confined to the sorting office in the mornings, but in the afternoons he escaped to collect the mail from the sub-post offices in the outlying Hertfordshire villages. Sometimes, during the school holidays, he would invite Jean or me to go with him. Of course this was against post-office rules, but this only made the outings seem much more exciting.

"Jump in," he'd say, opening the door of the van. "Quick – lie down under the mailbags and don't let anyone see you."

I would crouch down on the floor of the van under the mailbags until we had reached the safety of the countryside. It was then that our adventure really started.

There was only one seat in the van, so I had to sit on the floor on a couple of empty mailbags. We had no thought of seat belts – I don't think that they had been invented! The van was noisy and the roads very bumpy, but this all added to the excitement and pleasure. Nothing could spoil the outing. I was with Dad and we were both happy. He would smoke a precious Woodbine, which hung from his bottom lip when he spoke, and he would light each one from the stub of the last. No one had told us about pollution or lung disease, so we were happily ignorant of the consequences. Sadly, Dad died later from lung cancer – his life shortened by the pleasures he so much enjoyed in his younger days. He would always have a bag of boiled sweets for me to suck, saved from our weekly ration.

Our first stop was at a small village called Codicote, where the post office was housed in a small shop in the High Street. At every stop we were given something – a cup of tea, some cakes, eggs, apples, firewood – anything that the village postmaster could spare. Sometimes even a rabbit or a pheasant would be offered, and this was especially welcome in wartime. At Codicote there was always a steaming hot pot of tea waiting for us, and the tea would be served in the most enormous cups I have ever seen. It took ages to drink, and Dad would catch up

Chummy, our 'royal' cat.

with the village gossip, the weather, births and deaths. I was always included in the conversation, and this made me feel very grown-up.

"Did you hear about old Mrs Jarvis's son? Killed in France, he was – only been there two months. And what about Ted Jones' wife – expecting, she is. Disgusting I call it, and poor old Ted away fighting the war these past six months! God knows what he'll do when he finds out."

After Codicote we rattled through the lanes to Whitwell, stopping to gather conkers, acorns, crab apples or anything in season that looked interesting. At Whitwell (at least I think it was Whitwell – it's so many years ago) we would turn into a woodyard, as the post office was housed in a room in an adjoining cottage. Dad would show me round the yard. The noisy saws made it impossible to hear what he was saying. Enormous trees, ready for sawing, were brought to the woodyard on large lorries. It must have been extremely difficult manoeuvring these lorries through the narrow country lanes. The men were friendly, and we were soon covered in the sawdust which blew about the yard making the flowers and trees look a ghostly white. After another cup of tea, I would be given a bag of apples to munch; then we would say our goodbyes and be on our way.

One of the places we called at was St Paul's Walden Bury, the country home of the Queen Mother, then our queen.

"Stay there," Dad would say, "and don't get out of the van. Here's an apple to eat whilst I'm away. I won't be long."

And off he would go to collect the mail from the big house. Again I would crouch down on the floor of the van under the mailbags, but I couldn't resist peeping out of the van window at the beautiful house surrounded by colourful beds of flowers tended by a team of gardeners.

Dad was friendly with Jack, one of the gamekeepers, and one day he asked him if he knew where he could buy a kitten for Jean and me.

"There's a family of kittens in the barn, but they are wild," Jack told Dad, pointing to the barns nearby. "If you can catch one, you can have it."

Imagine our surprise and delight when Dad came home one day with a wriggling bundle in a mailbag – a little furry black and white kitten, which we christened Chummy. He had a cheeky white face and four tiny white paws. At first he was really wild, tearing around the living room and hiding under Dad's chair, but after a while he settled down. He grew into a really lovely cat and we had him for many years. We were especially proud as he had come from Queen ~~Elizabeth~~'s country home.   Mary's

Once we left Whitwell there were many other villages to visit: Preston, St Ippollitts, Gosmore, Offley, Pirton and Holwell, to name but a few. At the time when we visited them (the mid-1940s) they were real villages – no large housing estates or supermarkets, but rows of small cottages and a few council houses grouped around the village green. The village shops were stocked with everything imaginable. The postman was always a welcome visitor, and the village bobby was as important as the schoolmaster or the vicar. We weren't aware of much class distinction in the villages, although we always knew that the people living in the manor house or in the large houses tucked behind high hedges at the edge of the villages were not the same as us. They were obviously very rich. The church and the school were at the centre of all the activities, and the local pub was a meeting place for the men.

During our journeys in early summer we would pass by fields bright with buttercups and glimpse carpets of bluebells as the road skirted the woods. In the fields surrounding the farms there would be sheep with their tiny lambs enjoying the sunshine and cows chewing, contentedly resting between their twice-daily visits to the milking parlour. If the cows were lying down, rain was on the way, Dad said. At harvest time small tractors would pull the hay wagons, collecting the sheaves which had been stood in stooks until dry and then piled high into haystacks by farm workers with their pitchforks. Often this work was done by Land Girls, wearing their uniform of brown trousers and green jumpers.

Dad's van would gradually fill up with mailbags, which were piled high in the back until they spilled over into the front. I sat on them, which was much more comfortable than sitting on the floor.

Sadly, the afternoon's outing would come to an end when we arrived back in Hitchin. Dad would drop me off and return to the sorting office to offload the bags of mail. When I arrived back home, Mum and Jean would want to know how we had got on.

"What's in the bag?" Jean would ask. "Any apples?"

I would tell Mum if Dad was bringing a rabbit or eggs home, so that she could plan the next day's dinner. Tea would be ready on the table when Dad got home, and we would talk to each other about our afternoon's outing.

"Did you see the pheasants in the Queen's garden, and the rabbits, and did you see the fox hiding in the hedgerow at Offley and the ducks on the pond at Pirton?"

As we ate our watercress sandwiches or cheese on toast, which was always followed by home-made cake, I would snuggle up to Dad as we recalled our afternoon out.

"Come and help with the washing-up," Mum would interrupt us. "Then homework and bed!"

"Haven't got any homework," I would answer. "We're on holiday."

As I snuggled down under the eiderdown in our enormous bed, my thoughts would return to the country folk we had met earlier. Perhaps I'll be a postwoman when I grow up, or a school teacher in a village school, or I could join the Land Army, or – best of all – I could live like Queen Elizabeth in a big house with lots of servants.

How lucky I thought Dad was! He could drive around the villages every day. That would be much better than going to school – or so it seemed to me.

Going to Camp

"Mum, can we go to camp? Please, Mum, say yes."

Mum looked up from her knitting and placed the unfinished cardigan on the table. Jean and I rushed over to her. We had just returned from the Girls' Life Brigade meeting at the chapel.

"Captain says we can go to camp in August if you say so, for a week – it's only for a week. We can go, can't we?"

"You'll have to ask your dad" was Mum's reply.

"But he won't be home for ages." I wanted an answer immediately. "Dad's on nights – he won't be home till morning," I continued. "Please, Mum, *please*."

"Then you'll just have to wait, won't you?"

Mum picked up her knitting and the needles clicked furiously. We knew that Mum wouldn't make a decision without Dad, but we had to try.

"How much is this going to cost, and what sort of tent will you sleep in, and where is this camp?"

"It's not a proper camp, Mum – it's not in tents," I tried to reassure her. "We're going to stay in a bungalow on the beach; it belongs to Mr Halsey. It's near the King's home in Norfolk. It's called Snettisham." I stopped to get my breath back.

Mum looked relieved. Mr Halsey was one of the Sunday-school teachers, so it was probably all right. Jean and I had never before been away from home without our mother. The war had only ended the previous year and beaches had been out of bounds.

"Auntie Glad is going. She'll look after us."

Auntie Glad was an officer in the Girls' Life Brigade. Mum didn't look quite so anxious and the needles didn't click quite so fast.

"Well, that's different if your Auntie Glad is going, but you'll still have to ask Dad."

Mum checked her knitting pattern.

"Come on, you two – time for bed. You've got school in the morning."

Three months later, having got Dad's blessing, we were packed and ready to go. Two battered cases tied with string held our clothes and a few items of food and sweets (which were still in short supply and rationed).

"Hurry up or we'll miss the train."

I was impatient to get going. Our friend's father, who lived opposite, owned a car and we travelled in it to the railway station. This was a real treat as not many people owned a car in 1946. We waved to Mum through the rear window as the car moved slowly down the street.

"Mum's crying," Jean said. "What's she crying for?"

We stood in a small group on the platform at Hitchin Station, eagerly awaiting the train that would take us first to Cambridge and then on to the east coast. I can't remember where we got off the train, but Hunstanton was the nearest large town so it might have been there. Then a bus took us to the village of Snettisham, from where we had a long walk to our home for the next seven days.

Our accommodation was a wooden bungalow built at the top of the beach. There was nothing in front of the building but a vast expanse of sand and sea that seemed to stretch for miles and miles. The Wash was looking its best – calm, blue and inviting. We couldn't believe our luck. Little did we know that in the early 1950s the area would be devastated by floods and all the bungalows would be washed away.

Five of us had to sleep in the front bedroom in a double and a single bed. Most of us were used to sleeping with our brothers or sisters, so it didn't bother us. There were two adults in charge – the Captain and Auntie Glad – and two older girls were their helpers. I think that there were eight or nine girls altogether – quite a squash for a small bungalow!

It was heaven to be away from home, and we felt very grown-up. Neither the Captain nor Auntie Glad had children of their own, so we were allowed a freedom never dreamed of before.

When we awoke on the first morning a surprise awaited us: we looked out of the window and the sea had disappeared. It was nowhere to be seen – just miles of mud as far as the eye could see.

"Where's the sea gone?" we all wanted to know.

"It was full up last night."

"The tide's gone out," Auntie Glad explained. "It'll be back in soon."

Living in Central England, we had little knowledge of the ways of the sea. We were relieved when later that morning the tiny waves lapped against the beach and we were allowed to paddle. There were lots of shallow channels in the mud and sand when the tide went out, and pools which warmed up quickly in the sun. We had to make sure that when the tide started to come in we hurried back to the safety of the beach. This only added to the fun.

The adults did all the cooking in the tiny kitchen at the back of the bungalow. It was quite a squash sitting around the table. The food was basic, but we all enjoyed the fact that we were together with our friends. Nothing else mattered. The only catastrophe was when someone, who shall be nameless, used peppermint powder instead of milk powder. We still laugh about it sixty years later.

We had several outings during our stay, but the one that I remember best was a trip to Sandringham House, one of the homes of King George VI. We walked to the village, got a bus to the railway station, caught a train and then had quite a long walk, but the nearest we got to the house was outside the iron railings that surrounded the grounds. I don't remember seeing the actual house, but we were happy to think that the King sometimes stayed there. I do remember peering in through the railings, but I wonder now why the railings hadn't been taken away to make munitions for the war as most railings had been. Perhaps my memory is playing tricks, but I do remember peering in.

There was a tiny shop in the village of Snettisham – a wooden shack really – and we were allowed to walk there on our own and spend what small amounts of pocket money we had. We couldn't buy sweets as they were still rationed, but the shop sold an assortment of rubbishy goods and we would take ages deciding what to buy.

One day, midweek, we were returning from our daily unsupervised paddle in the mud and much to our surprise a car was parked next to the bungalow. Sitting close by at the top of the beach were our friend's parents and our mother. They had come to check up on us. They seemed somewhat upset when they didn't receive the welcome from us that they had expected. Jean and I tried to wipe away the mud from our legs, but to no avail. Our frocks, tucked into our knickers, were also covered in mud and creased beyond recognition. Mum didn't look pleased. I can still remember how annoyed I felt. Couldn't we be trusted on our own for one week?

One of the girls sharing our bedroom went to the local convent school. The rest of us either went to the secondary modern or Hitchin Girls' Grammar School. Funnily enough we accepted the grammar-school girls most of the time, but convent girls were an unknown quantity. Perhaps it was because their uniforms were brown and the rest of us wore navy blue. They also wore brown knickers.

The only lighting in the bungalow was by candles, and when we went to bed we used night lights. One particular night, with a flickering night light perched on our chest of drawers, we thoughtlessly pulled the door back until it met with the brown gabardine convent coat. It was a while before it became apparent that the smoke and smell should be investigated. We were slightly relieved that it was the convent coat that was damaged and not ours. It wasn't our convent friend that we didn't like but the brown convent uniform.

The week sadly came to an end much too quickly, but we had enjoyed our taste of freedom and would miss the companionship of our friends when we returned home. We were quieter on our return journey than we had been the previous week, but we had very happy memories, which remain with us to this day.

Praise the Lord!

Mum and Dad didn't profess to be religious, but from an early age Jean and I were sent to Sunday school. The nearest place of worship, just around the corner from our house, was Nightingale Road Methodist Chapel, where Auntie Glad and Auntie May belonged to the 'Sisterhood'.

The chapel was a stark building, as were most Methodist chapels. There were no stained-glass windows or statues – just plain wooden pews, a raised platform for the choir and a pulpit for the minister. On the left, next to the choir, was the organ – fed by a manual pump usually operated by one of the young boys. We would sometimes dare him to stop pumping every so often, and the lady organist would look very embarrassed when her musical efforts sounded squeaky and out of tune.

"Pump up! Pump up!" she would whisper, trying to catch his eye around the side of the organ.

As the boy got paid twopence a service he daren't stop pumping too often, especially as we girls in the choir were trying hard to suppress our laughter and the poor organist was getting angry and flustered.

As very young children we attended Sunday school both morning and afternoon attired in our Sunday best. We always looked forward to Easter Sunday as we usually wore new clothes. Mum would be busy for weeks beforehand, making new frocks for Jean and me, and we always had a knitted cardigan to match. Black patent Peggy shoes were a must, and rain or shine, warm or freezing cold, we left off our thick brown stockings, replacing them with white ankle socks. I still shiver at the thought. Straw hats adorned our heads, each with an artificial flower tucked into the ribbon. As soon as we arrived home, Mum would meet us in the scullery.

"Take your best clothes off quickly," she would say. "Fold them up neatly, then you can lay the table."

We would put on our old clothes, eat our dinner and put our best clothes on again for afternoon Sunday school. In those wartime days children didn't wear jeans and tee shirts – they hadn't been invented! Our play clothes consisted of frocks made by Mum out of our aunties' old cast-offs.

The chapel provided us with a very good way to keep out of mischief by keeping us occupied. Monday night was Girls' Life Brigade. We would dress up in our navy uniforms, complete with hat. We would work hard to win badges – sewing, first aid, general knowledge, country dancing and many more. All the badges were sewn on to the sleeves of our serge uniforms, so the garments could never be washed. The minister's wife was captain, and there were three other officers – one of which was Auntie Glad. When we arrived we would be lined up and drilled.

"Form a line!" the Captain would call out. "Tallest on the left and shortest on the right in two ranks!"

There would be much shuffling, pushing and arguing about who was tallest and who wasn't, but finally we would get it right. We would learn how to juggle clubs, skip and dance – it was all good fun.

Tuesday night was choir practice – the choir was made up entirely of girls. We would gather to sing familiar hymns and learn new ones accompanied by a very old upright piano played by Miss Adkins. After choir practice we would play games. 'Keys' was one of our favourites. In this game one person was blindfolded and we all sat on the floor in a circle. A bunch of

Nightingale Road Methodist Chapel before the front porch was built.

keys would be quietly placed on the floor, and the blindfolded person would have to point at another girl before she could retrieve the keys. It doesn't sound very exciting now, but we enjoyed it.

Once we were at senior school we were allowed to join the youth club, which met on Wednesdays. This was the best night of the week. We felt very grown-up as we played table tennis and darts and drank coffee whilst we discussed the best way to solve the world's problems. Some of the local boys were joined by a few lads from the nearby RAF camp at Henlow. The Methodist Association of Youth Clubs held an annual conference weekend at the Royal Albert Hall, consisting of displays, singing by various choirs from all over the UK, and a netball match. It took me many weeks of discussion with the organisers to convince them that, although we were only a very small youth club, we could muster a great netball team.

The youth-club netball team at the Royal Albert Hall.

Eventually they agreed, and we turned up with our short red skirts and white Aertex shirts in our carrier bags. We didn't win, but we took part.

Once a year we put on a variety concert for the chapel congregation. This consisted of all kinds of acts. Jean and I sang and acted 'We're a Couple of Swells' and 'Pedro the Fisherman', and six of us performed 'We'll Gather Lilacs' in dresses and hoops made from mauve crêpe paper. I cringe now at the memory, but the church hall was always packed with people prepared to pay twopence for the experience, which included tea and biscuits.

The chapel year was made up of various celebrations. Apart from wearing new clothes I always enjoyed the Easter service and hymns. At eight o'clock on Easter Sunday the BBC news would start with the hymn 'Christ the Lord Is Risen Today'.

'If the BBC believes that, it's good enough for me,' I thought.

Sadly that hymn doesn't start Easter Sunday any more.

In midsummer we celebrated the chapel anniversary, and a great effort went into the special services. We would learn new hymns and perform readings and plays, and the grown-ups would wear new hats. I remember one lady who wore a hat decorated with a red feather bird; it entered the chapel before she did! The Sisterhood would sing at the evening service, and this was always very good entertainment. Auntie May would sometimes sing a solo, and her rendering of 'Oh for the Wings of a Dove' in a quivering voice would send Jean and me into fits of laughter, hiding behind our hymn books.

The harvest festival was my favourite. Everyone would take either flowers, fruit or vegetables to decorate the chapel.

"What can we take, Dad?" we would ask. "What about that enormous cabbage or a bunch of carrots?"

All contributions were gathered from the congregation's gardens – it was unheard of for anyone to buy any type of produce. Every window in the chapel would be crammed full of our offerings, and I always thought that it was the only time of the year when the chapel actually looked beautiful.

Christmas was a very exciting time for us, both at home and at the chapel. We enjoyed singing carols, and I still remember a carol sung by the son of one of our ministers. It went like this:

When darkness creeps over the sea
And hides our fair land far from sight,
What will our sailors do then?
Who'll keep them safe through the night?

Then it went on about the dark rocks and the dangers, and asked who would light up their way and guide them home. Well, we all knew who would save them from harm – everything was so simple in those days.

After Christmas Sunday celebrations, we would perform a nativity play. I was never chosen to be Mary – I was too tall. I was always a shepherd or wise man, complete with a tea towel tied around my head or a paper crown. I remember wearing either a tunic made from an old sheet or old curtains, depending on the character. Very occasionally I was an angel, and I would wear the same sheet with cardboard wings. Dad would make me a halo from a length of wire decorated with tinsel. I still remember feeling really upset when one or other of my friends was chosen to be Mary. Once I was chosen to play the part of Joseph, but that upset me even more.

The chapel played a very important part in my childhood. As well as teaching me about the rights and wrongs of life, it taught me to think for myself.

"If a thing's worth doing, it's worth doing well," my Sunday-school teacher told me one day when I showed her a school dress that I was making, badly.

I never forgot that.

I also rarely drink alcohol – Methodists are supposed to be teetotal.

The week before my marriage I was confirmed into the Church

of England. I was really scared about telling the Methodist minister, but he reassured me, saying, "The Church of England could do with some good Methodists."

Sadly the chapel and schoolrooms were demolished many years ago to make room for new developments. Why is it that so many interesting buildings that were so important to me during my childhood are no more? I guess it's called progress, but that's not what I call it.

My Girl's Life Brigade badges.

A Really Lovely Holiday

"Jean, Molly, come inside. I've got something to tell you."

We hurried in from the garden and into the living room, wondering what had happened. Dad sounded really excited, which was a fairly rare event.

"What's the matter, Dad? What's happened?"

We joined Mum, who was sitting down at the wooden table. She looked pleased.

"We're going on holiday, that's what's the matter." Dad held a letter in his hand and waved it in the air. "We're going to Hastings for a fortnight."

We'd never seen Dad so excited.

It was the spring of 1946. The war was over and beaches were being opened up again. During the war most beaches were surrounded by barbed wire and patrolled by soldiers or the Home Guard, so no one was able to go away to the seaside, especially to the south-east coast.

"When are we going? How are we going to get there? Where are we going to stay?" Jean stopped to get her breath.

I turned to Dad: "Where's Hastings?" I asked.

Dad got out his pen and a piece of paper and drew a rough outline of England.

"That's Hastings," he said: "between Dover and Eastbourne. It's on the south coast."

"Is there a beach," I asked, "and lots of sand? Can we swim in the sea and go out in a boat?"

"Why do you have to ask so many questions?" Dad looked a bit grumpy, but he added, "I don't know about the beach, but there's a castle and cliffs and we're going by train."

Jean and I looked at each other. We couldn't believe that we would be travelling all that way by train. The longest train journey that we could remember going on as a family was to Granny Foster's at Welwyn Garden City some twelve miles away.

"We'll get the train to London and another from London to Hastings. It'll take about five hours."

Dad was looking pleased again, and Mum was already making plans.

"We'll need two cases for our clothes and another one for our food." Food was still rationed but you could spend two weeks' coupons to buy rations in another town. "We mustn't forget to take our ration books. I'll start saving tins and packets of food. Mrs Watts, the Hastings landlady, has promised to cook for us, but we have to provide the food."

Jean and I weren't interested in buying food. We were too excited to think about anything except the train journey and the beach. We had been to the sea as very young children. We could remember day trips to Margate, playing on the sandy beach with Auntie May and Auntie Glad, but we had always returned home at night.

The weeks before our school broke up for the summer holidays dragged slowly on. Jean and I made plans, mostly about the beach and the sea. We were both good swimmers, but our only swimming experiences had been at the open-air swimming pool in Hitchin.

At last the day arrived to leave for our holiday. The night before we had dragged the tin bath from its nail and we had washed ourselves and our hair and had our weekly dose of syrup of figs.

"Early to bed!" Mum had told us. "We're getting up early

tomorrow to catch the train. Get to sleep quickly, and no talking."

Dad had packed the suitcases, and we had helped by sitting on them so that Dad could fasten them. String was tied around them to stop them from bursting open. The suitcase carrying our rations was full. It was so heavy that it was almost impossible to lift. Needless to say, Jean and I were too excited to get much sleep.

It seemed no time at all until we heard Dad's alarm clock going off.

"Hurry up! Get dressed!"

We washed ourselves at the sink in the scullery as Mum cooked our breakfast. Swiftly we ate our boiled eggs and bread and butter, wondering where we would eat our next meal. At eight thirty Dad looked at his watch. A knock at the front door made us jump. No one used our front door, except the doctor.

"Taxi for Mr Kitchener."

Jean and I looked at each other, hardly believing our ears. We'd never been in a taxi before; we'd rarely even been in a car.

The taxi driver took the two lighter cases, put them in the boot of his taxi and then returned for the third.

"Wot you got in 'ere, mate," he asked Dad, "the Crown Jewels?"

Dad laughed. "That's our food for the next two weeks," he told the driver. "Mum's been saving up for months."

The neighbours were looking out of their front-room windows. We felt really grand. Dad must have saved up for ages for this holiday.

It took only about five minutes to reach Hitchin Station. We got out of the taxi and helped Mum with the two lighter cases. Dad paid the taxi driver, who lifted the heavy case out and deposited it in the road.

"Rather you than me, mate," he told Dad. "Hope you have a good 'oliday."

Dad, who was a very small man, struggled into the booking hall and bought our tickets. A porter watched him from the platform. The London train went from the opposite platform, which was reached by an underpass. The porter obviously felt sorry for Dad and fetched his hand barrow.

"'Ere you are, mate."

He helped Dad put the three cases on and pushed them towards the end of the platform.

"You take your missus and kids down the steps and I'll meet you at the other side."

When we reached the London platform the porter had wheeled his barrow across the rails and was waiting for us.

The train journey was really exciting. As well as passing through the beautiful Hertfordshire countryside we could see into the rooms and back gardens of people's homes. A couple of soldiers shared our carriage and helped Dad with our luggage at King's Cross. We took another taxi across London and were soon speeding on our way to the coast.

"The first one to see the sea is the winner," Jean called out.

We were so excited. What did the English Channel look like? We wondered whether we would be able to see the edge of the water on the other side. We looked out of the open window, smoke from the steam engine making our eyes water.

"I can see the sea! I can see the sea!" Jean called out.

"I saw it first," I said. "I saw it a few minutes ago."

"No, you didn't," Jean retorted.

"I did."

"Stop arguing, you two." Dad couldn't put up with us arguing. "We're on holiday."

We all gazed at the large expanse of blue.

"It goes on for ever," I gasped: "for miles and miles."

The train came to a halt.

"Hastings. This is Hastings," a porter called out. "All change!"

We had arrived. The rest of the day passed in a haze. Another taxi took us to Harold Road, where we were welcomed by our landlady, Mrs Watts. She looked like a jolly, cuddly person.

"Dinner's ready," she told us. "We'll sort out your rooms and rations later."

After dinner we were shown our bedrooms. Jean and I shared a double bed in the back room – it looked just like our room at home except that it boasted an electric light. I switched it on and off to make sure it worked. Next to the bedroom there was a bathroom. Jean turned the tap on at the sink and hot water ran out.

'No washing in cold water for two weeks!' I thought. 'This is going to be a lovely holiday.'

Mrs Watts' home was about a mile from the beach at the top of a very steep hill. The walk to the beach each day took no time at all as we were eager to reach the delights of the seashore. Coming back at midday for dinner was a different matter, though, as it was uphill all the way. We passed the lovely buildings of Hastings Old Town, but we had to carry the extra food bought in the town shops and it was tiring. When dinner was over we walked back down to the beach, and then we walked back again at teatime.

The two weeks spent in Hastings was a wonderful time for us all. We'd never been together with Mum and Dad for so long. At home Dad worked long hours as a postman, and at night, during the war, he had been on call as a head warden. Together we walked along the cliffs, explored the fish markets and even went on a day visit to Eastbourne.

Hastings Beach was full of large pebbles at high tide, but when the tide went out huge stretches of sand were exposed, with warm rock pools where we searched for crabs.

"Where does the sea go to?" I asked Dad one day at low tide. "It looks as though someone has pulled the plug out."

Dad remained silent.

'I don't suppose he knows,' I thought. 'I'll have to ask my teacher,' I decided.

One day when it was too rough to swim, Jean and I went for a boat trip. I can still remember the small boat rising and falling as the waves broke over the sides, wetting us. It was wonderful.

The last day of our holiday Dad decided as a treat to take us to a fish-and-chip restaurant. It was our first experience of eating out, and we sat down and enjoyed the tasty fresh fish and crispy chips. When Dad got up to pay the bill, he turned pale. The food cost twice as much as he had expected. After we had walked out of the door and round the corner, we found out why. We had entered through the back door. The front entrance, on the seafront, was very posh. 'Café de Milo' it said in large capital letters. Dad was not amused. I still laugh when we drive past – it's still a fish-and-chip restaurant.

Sadly, too soon our holiday came to an end, and we packed our suitcases ready for the return journey. The food case was much lighter – we'd eaten most of its contents. We said goodbye to Mrs Watts and her husband, who worked in a draper's shop in Hastings.

"Come again next year," he called out as the taxi drove slowly down the hill.

"Yes please," Jean and I shouted in unison. "Can we, Dad?"

The journey home was enjoyable – the train puffed its way through towns and countryside until at last we arrived back in Hitchin.

"Hitchin. This is Hitchin. Change here for Cambridge."

"I wish we were just going instead of coming home," I told Dad. "Do you really think we'll be able to go again next year?"

"We'll see," Dad replied.

'Why do grown-ups always say, "We'll see," when they don't want to give a straight answer?' I wondered.

Tired out, Jean and I undressed for bed.

"You've got a white cross on your back," Jean shrieked out.

"So have you," I told her. "It's where the straps on our swimming costumes went."

"Go to sleep," Mum called up the stairs. "No more talking!"

"Goodnight, Jean."

"Goodnight, Molly."

"Wasn't it a lovely holiday?" I said sleepily.

"Yes," Jean yawned, "a very lovely holiday."

Mum and Dad on holiday at Southsea.

Time to Grow Up

In the 1940s children grew up quickly. Except for the fortunate few who had been educated at grammar schools and went on to university, most children left school at fourteen or fifteen and were sent out to work. Their future was planned out for them: leave school, get a job, find a boyfriend or girlfriend; then, after a period of courting and an engagement, get married and have children. This is what we expected to happen to us, and most of my friends, like me, were happy to follow this plan. Our expectations were limited. Parents encouraged this way of thinking and were pleased to have the extra money that their children's employment brought in.

This book is about my childhood, so I do not wish to delve into my life after that period, but I do want to look back and try to understand how my childhood prepared me for life.

Reading through the chapters and talking about it with my grandchildren has been like going on a wonderful journey. Growing up during the Second World War certainly influenced my whole life. I have talked to my sister about certain episodes in my story, and it has been interesting to note that she remembers some of our experiences in a very different way. We remember good and bad times, but we both agreed that our childhood was a very happy one. Although our formative years took place during the war, we always felt sure that we would win the war – there was never any question about that – and as we had never experienced the 'good old days' we didn't

Me, as a teenager.

miss them. Rationing was something that Mum took care of, and our safety was in Dad's hands.

My grandchildren cannot understand how we managed without a bathroom, hot water, electricity, a car, a TV, a mobile phone or a computer. They pull faces when I tell them about our lavatory up the garden and the chamber pot under the bed; how we shook with fear when the siren sounded, and how we took shelter in the cupboard under the stairs. It was difficult for young women to have to manage without stockings and make-up and during the war, and many jumped into marriage in a hurry, only to find that mistakes had been made. Fortunately I was too young to worry about this.

How did growing up in the 1930s and 1940s affect the rest of my life? Certainly it made me appreciate the luxuries that were denied us during and immediately after the war. Food rationing began in 1940 and continued for some time after the end of hostilities. It seemed a very long time before things improved, and it wasn't until 1953 that sweet rationing ended.

My parents' generation found it difficult to forgive the enemy as they had been affected badly, but I think that my generation were quicker to forgive. Many families had lost loved ones and their homes, but we were lucky as no one from our family was killed and only a few bombs fell on Hitchin.

Gradually we returned to normal. Looking back, I think that the conditions and experiences of my childhood made me appreciate the ordinary things of life – living without the fear of air raids, no rationing, street lamps that were turned on and blackouts discarded. I am still cautious about turning on our electric lights, and I still revel in a bath full of hot water and unrestricted food-shopping.

I don't regret being born when I was. Life was much simpler then. We didn't have many material possessions, so we made our own fun. We were really inventive, and we were content with our way of life. We weren't restricted like most young children are today, and we didn't expect expensive toys or presents. How would my life have differed if I had been born much later? I'll never know, but I wouldn't have had to struggle with a mobile phone or DVDs. I'll never fully understand how to work them.

What do I remember most vividly? Mantles and matches, caterpillars and rag-and-bone men, the tin bath in the scullery and syrup of figs; or was it the lavatory in the barn, the Methodist chapel and those awful concerts. These will always be a part of my childhood – a childhood to remember and cherish.

Me as a teenager.